BEGINNINGS

Senior Authors
Carl B. Smith
Virginia A. Arnold

Linguistics Consultant
Ronald Wardhaugh

Macmillan Publishing Co., Inc.
New York
Collier Macmillan Publishers
London

Copyright © 1983 Macmillan Publishing Co., Inc.

All rights reserved. No part of this book may be reproduced or transmitted in any form or by any means, electronic or mechanical, including photocopying, recording, or by any information storage and retrieval system, without permission in writing from the Publisher.

This work is also published together with other works in a single volume under the title: *Full Circle,* copyright © 1983 Macmillan Publishing Co., Inc. Parts of this work were published in earlier editions of SERIES r.

Macmillan Publishing Co., Inc.
866 Third Avenue, New York, New York 10022
Collier Macmillan Canada, Inc.

Printed in the United States of America
ISBN 0-02-132050-0
9 8 7 6 5 4 3 2 1

ACKNOWLEDGMENTS

The publisher gratefully acknowledges permission to reprint the following copyrighted material:

"Butterfly Wings," from *In the Woods, In the Meadow, In the Sky* by Aileen Fisher. Copyright © 1965 by Aileen Fisher. Reprinted by permission of Charles Scribner's Sons.

"Don't tell me that I talk too much," from *And the Frog Went Blah* by Arnold Spilka. Copyright © 1972 by Arnold Spilka. Reprinted by permission of Charles Scribner's Sons.

"The Girl Who Found a Dragon," from *Dinosaurs* by Darlene Geis. Copyright © 1969 by Grosset & Dunlap, Inc. Published by Grosset & Dunlap, Inc.

"Harlequin and the Gift of Many Colors," adapted from *Harlequin and the Gift of Many Colors* by Remy Charlip and Burton Supree. Copyright © 1973 by Remy Charlip and Burton Supree. All rights reserved. Published by Parents' Magazine Press. Reprinted by permission of Arthur D. Zinberg, Esq., 11 East 44th Street, New York, New York 10017.

"Margarita's Gift" by Ann Devendorf from *Highlights for Children,* August/September 1977. Copyright © 1977, Highlights for Children, Inc. All rights reserved.

"Pablo Picasso: His Younger Years," by Nancy White from *Highlights for Children,* October 1972. Copyright © Highlights for Children, Inc., Columbus, Ohio. All rights reserved.

"The River Is a Piece of Sky," from *The Reason for the Pelican* by John Ciardi. Copyright © 1959 by John Ciardi. Reprinted by permission of J.B. Lippincott Company.

"The Rooster Who Understood Japanese," from *The Rooster Who Understood Japanese* by Yoshiko Uchida. Copyright © 1976 by Yoshiko Uchida. Reprinted by permission of Charles Scribner's Sons.

"Simon Boom Gives a Wedding," adapted from *Simon Boom Gives a Wedding* by Yuri Suhl. Copyright © 1972 by Yuri Suhl. Reprinted by permission of Four Winds Press, a division of Scholastic Magazines, Inc. and Joan Daves.

"Walter In Love," adapted from *Walter In Love* by Alicen White. Copyright © 1973 by Alicen White. Adapted by permission of Alicen White: Frieda Fishbein, Ltd., Author's Agent.

"You, you, caribou," from *Songs and Stories of the Netsilik Eskimo,* translated by Edward Field, published as part of the upper elementary school course *Man: A Course of Study,* developed by the Social Studies Program of EDC under a grant from the National Science Foundation. Copyright © 1967, 1968 EDC, Inc. Used with permission.

Illustrations: Ray Cruz, pp. 4-7; Len Ebert, pp. 10-21; Jan Pyk, pp. 22-29; Pat Steward, pp. 34-61; John Melo, pp. 62-63; David Brown, pp. 64-77; Donald Gates, pp. 78-83; Remy Charlip, pp. 86-103; Anna Graf, pp. 104-115; David McPhail, pp. 116-125; David Blanchette, pp. 126-127; Betty Fraser, pp. 128-141; Frank Bozzo, pp. 142-143; Vladimir Hervert, pp. 144-151; Sven Lindman, pp. 152-153; Gordon Laite, pp. 156-177; M. (Kiki) Janovitz, pp. 178-181. **Photographs:** Ralph Hunt Williams (Bruce Coleman Inc.), pp. 30-31; Anna Graf, pp. 107-112.

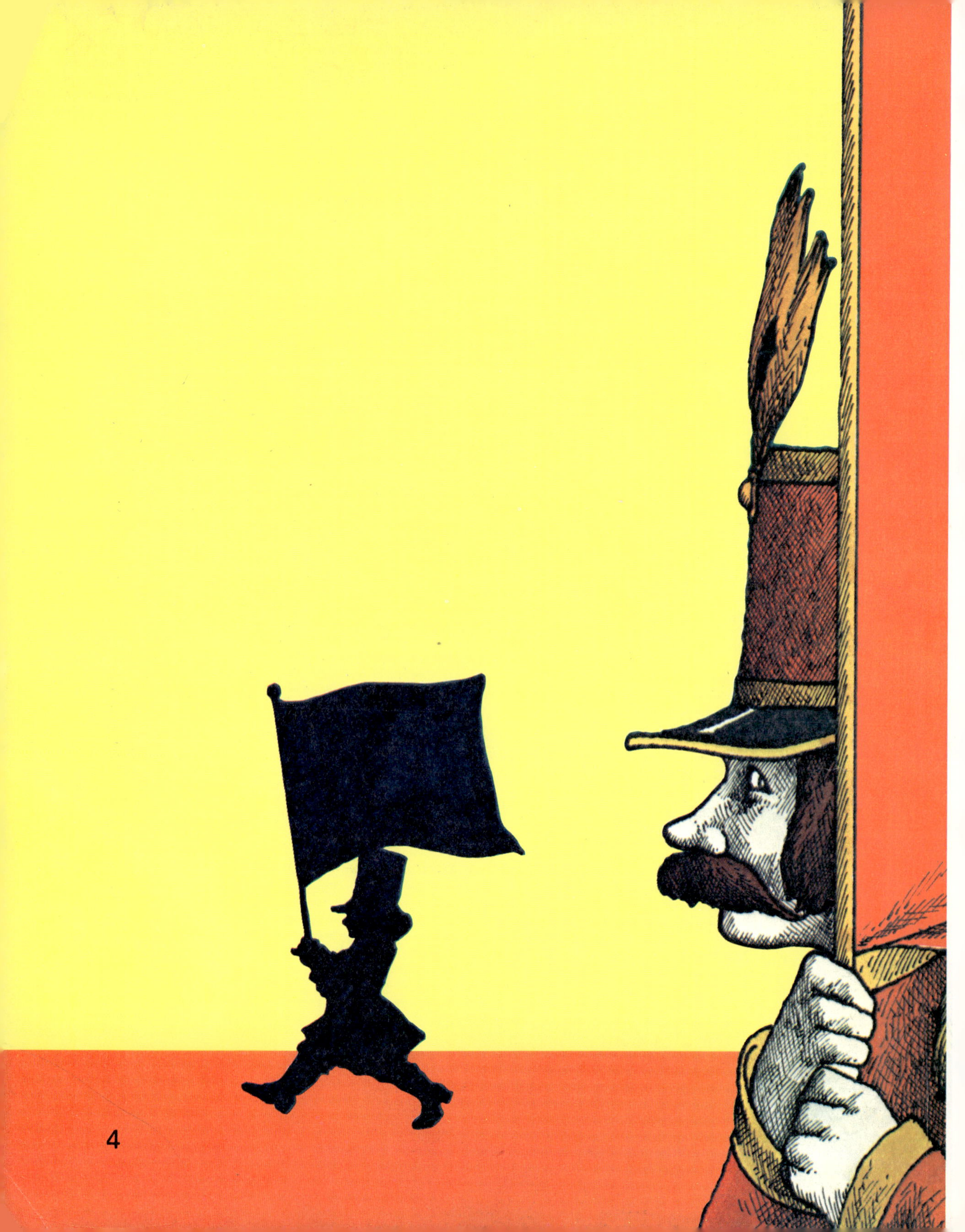

Contents

Introduction to BEGINNINGS 9

Phoebe's First Duet, a story by Judith Davis 10

What's the Matter with Thurman? a story by
Dina Anastasio 22

You, You, Caribou, an Eskimo poem 30

SKILLS: **How Did the Writer Feel?**
(Author's Point of View) 32

The Rooster Who Understood Japanese, a story
by Yoshiko Uchida
Mr. Lincoln's Crowing 34
A Box for Mr. Lincoln 45
Mr. Lincoln's New Home 53

Butterfly Wings, a poem by Aileen Fisher 62

Hot Enough for You? a story by Elizabeth Levy
The Hydrant 64
Erica the Inventor 70

Margarita's Gift, a story by Ann Devendorf 78

SKILLS: **What's the Meaning of This?**
(Multiple-Meaning Words) 84

Harlequin and the Gift of Many Colors, a story
by Remy Charlip and Burton Supree
Only a Blanket 86
A Piece of Cloth 94

Pablo Picasso, a biographical sketch by Nancy White
His Younger Years 104
A Very Famous Artist 111

Walter in Love, a story by Alicen White 116

Don't Tell Me That I Talk Too Much! a poem
by Arnold Spilka 126

The Friendship Game, a story by Dina Anastasio 128

The River Is a Piece of Sky, a poem by John Ciardi ... 142

The Girl Who Found a Dragon, an article by
Darlene Geis ... 144

Famous Firsts, items from the Guinness Book
of World Records ... 152

SKILLS: Watch Out! (Homographs) ... 154

Simon Boom Gives a Wedding, a story by Yuri Suhl
Only the Best ... 156
The Very Best ... 167

Over in the Meadow, a poem by Olive A. Wadsworth ... 178

SKILLS: Before and After
(Prefixes and Suffixes) ... 182

Conclusion for BEGINNINGS ... 184

Glossary ... 185

BEGINNINGS

When you have finished one thing, it's time to start something new. Sometimes something you do may not work right. Then it's time to start over. There are always new ways to do things. If you think about the things you do, you may find new ways to do these things.

In "Beginnings," you will read about a girl and her grandfather who try something new. You will read about two girls who speak different languages and find a way to talk to each other. As you read, see if you can think of other ways to do the things you read about. Would your way work as well?

Phoebe's First Duet

Judith Davis

I never missed a party at Grandpa Theo's. All my aunts, uncles, and cousins were there. All Grandpa Theo's friends and music pupils came, too.

The table was covered with good food. People talked and laughed and sang. Sometimes Uncle Dimitri pulled out his handkerchief. He took Aunt Myra's hand, and Grandpa Theo took Grandma's hand. Then they did the snake dance. We all joined hands and lined up behind them. We wound in and out, dancing the slow snake dance.

Then Grandpa Theo opened the piano. Everyone was quiet. "Phoebe," he called to me, "please turn the pages for us."

Grandpa Theo sat down with one of his pupils. They played wonderful music together, while I turned the pages. I was learning to play the piano with Grandpa Theo, so that someday I would be ready to play a duet with him.

But then things changed. I knew something was wrong when Grandpa didn't have music parties very often. Grandpa Theo didn't sing and he didn't dance. His pupils played duets without him. When the parties stopped for good, I knew something was really wrong. Later, even my piano lessons stopped.

Grandpa Theo didn't like to talk about it. But I knew he had trouble hearing. If he didn't watch me when I talked, he sometimes wouldn't even answer me. Other times he wouldn't laugh when I said something funny.

He turned the radio on too loudly. People had to shout when they wanted to talk to him. I had to pat his shoulder to get him to look at me when I talked. But he just didn't talk with me very much any more.

Whenever we visited Grandpa Theo, my mother would say, "Papa, why don't you go get a hearing test? Maybe you need a hearing aid."

But Grandpa wouldn't go. He wouldn't listen to her. One day, when we were visiting, my mother told him again to get a hearing test.

Grandpa Theo said, "I have always taken care of myself. I'll go on taking care of myself, too. Anyway, why should I look foolish?"

"You wouldn't look foolish, Papa," my mother said. "It's not foolish to hear better." But Grandpa didn't hear her. He went out to the garden to be alone.

I felt very sad. "I wish Grandpa Theo could hear better," I told my mother. "I really miss all the things we used to do together."

"Why don't you go out and tell him that, Phoebe?" my mother asked.

So I went out to the garden. I found Grandpa Theo sitting under the fig tree, looking up at the pretty leaves. I patted his shoulder. He looked at me.

"Grandpa Theo, I really miss our talks and your songs and your parties. I miss my piano lessons, too. Maybe a hearing aid would help you hear better, and we could do those things again. Why won't you even try?"

Grandpa Theo stared at me. It was so quiet in the garden that I could hear a leaf fall from the tree.

"Maybe you're right, Phoebe," he said slowly. "I could try. I guess I was thinking only of myself." Then he smiled at me and took my hand. "Are you still playing the piano?" he asked.

"Yes, Grandpa Theo, but it's not the same."

"Do you remember to play one hand at a time, and then both hands together?"

"Yes, Grandpa Theo."

"Do you play each piece slowly at first?" he asked.

"Sometimes," I said, "but I like to play fast."

"Yes, you play well," Grandpa Theo said. "You should be ready for a duet soon."

Something inside me jumped. For a minute I couldn't say a thing. I just looked at Grandpa Theo.

"Pheobe," said Grandpa Theo, "I miss your lessons, too. I just wasn't thinking about the important things. But now I'm going to get a hearing test, and I'd like you to come with me."

"Oh, Grandpa Theo!" I shouted, and I gave him a big hug. I felt like singing.

"If a hearing aid can help," he said, "you shall play your first duet soon."

Three days later, we went to see Dr. Grant. She asked Grandpa a lot of questions. Then she gave Grandpa some earphones.

"These earphones will test your hearing," she said. "I'll test one ear at a time. As soon as you can hear a sound in the earphones, press this button." She showed Grandpa Theo where the button was.

"Then I'll make the sound louder, so you can hear it very well," Dr. Grant said. "After that, I'll make it softer and softer, until you can't hear it any more. I'll do this many times, until I know just when you start to hear the sound. Are you ready?"

Grandpa Theo nodded and put the earphones on. I smiled at him.

Dr. Grant gave Grandpa Theo a lot of different tests. When they were all done, she sat down to talk with us again.

"You are lucky," she said. "A hearing aid makes sounds louder. Right now, that's all you need to hear better."

Grandpa Theo gave a big sigh and smiled. Then Dr. Grant showed him all the different kinds of hearing aids. One of them looked like a little radio. It had wires coming out of it, with little earplugs at the ends of the wires.

Another one could be put onto eyeglasses, and another one went on the back of the ear.

Dr. Grant gave Grandpa the kind that looked like a radio. "Try this one."

"This doesn't look so bad," said Grandpa Theo. "Phoebe, go to the other side of the room and say something, and I will try my new hearing aid."

"When can we start playing?" I asked from the other side of the room.

"Today!" cried Grandpa Theo. "I can hear you very well! We've got a lot of work to do. You must get ready for your first duet."

"May I listen through your hearing aid?" I asked.

Grandpa Theo looked at Dr. Grant. She nodded, so Grandpa gave me the hearing aid. I listened through it. It really made everything sound loud. Then I gave it back to Grandpa Theo.

"You must go slowly at first," said Dr. Grant, smiling. "Wear the hearing aid a little longer each day, until you are used to it. Take good care of it, and it will work well for you, like any other tool. Good luck with your duet. Let me know how you do."

"Thank you, Dr. Grant," said Grandpa Theo. We shook hands all around.

Grandpa Theo used the hearing aid a little longer each day. "It helps me when I'm playing the piano," he said. "But it picks up all kinds of sounds. Sudden sounds or loud ones are hard to take.

When there are too many loud sounds at once, I just turn it off."

In time, Grandpa Theo got used to his hearing aid. He began to like it very much.

During that time, I learned my first duet. We played the duet for everyone at Grandpa Theo's next music party. This time, one of my cousins turned the pages!

WHAT'S THE MATTER WITH THURMAN?

Dina Anastasio

Thurman's life was very good. The pond in which he lived was clean and cool. The countryside was peaceful and quiet. And, best of all, Thurman had more friends than he knew what to do with.

Oh, he had problems, of course, for he was very small, like all tadpoles. Snakes, fish, and even frogs, were always trying to catch him for dinner. But they never caught Thurman. He was much too fast and clever for them.

Thurman was the biggest and the smartest of all the tadpoles in the pond. And he soon became the leader.

Day after day, hour after hour, Thurman swam up and down the pond in search of something to eat.

And, always, the other tadpoles followed him.

"If anyone can find a water plant to munch on," they said, "Thurman can!"

So you can imagine why Thurman was so well thought of in his peaceful pond.

Up and down they swam, hiding from enemies and searching for food. As they swam, they drank mouthfuls of water. The water passed back through the gills inside their heads. In this way they breathed, taking air from the water with their gills. Then they blew the water out of holes on the side of their heads—just like a fish.

When Thurman was about two months old, a strange thing happened. He was swimming along one peaceful day in search of food. All of a sudden the sound of laughter echoed behind him. Of course, tadpoles don't really laugh, so you'll have to imagine a little bit here. It was clear to Thurman that *something* was strange.

Shaking his tail, Thurman flipped around and faced his friends.

"What's so funny?" Thurman asked, smiling, for he was always ready for a good laugh.

But no one answered. They just sat there, staring at Thurman. Then they all swam away.

Poor Thurman! He had no idea what was wrong. But that something was indeed wrong was *very* clear.

Thurman was miserable! All day long he swam around alone. He thought about the other tadpoles who had once been his friends.

Toward dark, a tiny little tadpole swam up to Thurman.

"Hi, Thurman!" he said.

"I thought no one was speaking to me," said Thurman sadly.

The little tadpole had not heard of Thurman's troubles, and so he stayed to play. But it was not long before he too noticed something odd about Thurman. Then he began to laugh.

"What *is* it?" cried Thurman.

The little tadpole laughed and laughed. His tail shook and he swam round and round. At last he stopped and turned to Thurman.

"*Things,*" he cried, "are growing under your tail! They look like little stumps. What's the matter with you, Thurman?"

And then, without waiting for an answer, the little tadpole swam away.

Poor Thurman! He didn't know what was happening to him. He flicked his tail and—yes—something was indeed growing under his tail.

Although Thurman didn't know it, something wonderful was happening to him.

Thurman Tadpole was becoming a frog! And those two little stumps were the beginnings of what would soon become two nice long legs.

But of course *Thurman* didn't know any of this. All Thurman knew was that he was now different from the other tadpoles. He was very lonely.

And so poor Thurman played alone for what seemed like forever, but was really only about a month.

And throughout it all, Thurman changed. As his back legs grew, his front legs began to form behind the gills under his skin. One day one of these front legs popped out of his gill hole. This really made the other tadpoles laugh.

"What's the matter with Thurman?" they asked as he began to look stranger and stranger.

The more he changed, the more unhappy poor Thurman became. The other tadpoles either laughed at him or didn't speak to him at all.

And Thurman's life was miserable.

Thurman was *very* unhappy.

Soon Thurman's other leg popped out. He began to look more and more like a frog. But Thurman wasn't only changing on the outside.

He was also becoming a frog on the inside.

His gills changed to lungs, which meant that Thurman had to swim up to breathe air. His mouth became bony, so that he would be able to eat bugs instead of water plants. While this was happening, Thurman didn't eat at all. He lived on food which was stored in his tail. As Thurman's teeth formed, his tail shrank until, at last, it was a stump. Thurman had become a frog!

Of course, by this time, all of the other tadpoles had changed, too. But not one had changed as much as Thurman. So they still laughed and asked, "What's the matter with Thurman?" And Thurman was very sad!

One day, when Thurman's tail had disappeared and his skin had turned dark green, he decided to try out his new legs. With one big jump, he hopped out of the water and onto a nearby rock. With his big eyes he took in the world around him. Then he looked down into the water at the tadpoles who used to be his friends. And, for the first time in his life, Thurman felt sorry for someone other than himself. They too would soon discover this wonderful world outside their pond. But right now they were still, in many ways, just fish. But he—Thurman Tadpole—was a fine, fat frog!

Thurman laughed and waved, and with one very high jump, he hopped off to explore his new world.

YOU, YOU, CARIBOU

The caribou is a kind of deer that the Eskimos have depended on for many years. This poem about a caribou is by an Eskimo hunter. It was spoken to a Danish man who wrote it down in his own language. Later, the poem was changed into English, the language we speak.

30

You, you, caribou
yes you
    long legs
yes you
    long ears
you with the long neck hair—
From far off you're little as a louse;
Be my swan, fly to me, long horns
waving great bull
    cari-bou-bou-bou.

Put your footprints on this land,
this land I'm standing on,
So rich with the lichens you love.
See, I'm holding in my hand
the reindeer moss you're dreaming of—
So delicious yum, yum, yum—
Come, caribou, come.

Come on, move those bones,
move your leg bones back and forth
and give yourself to me.
I'm here,
I'm waiting just for you
you, you, caribou.
APPEAR.
COME HERE.
        —An Eskimo Poem

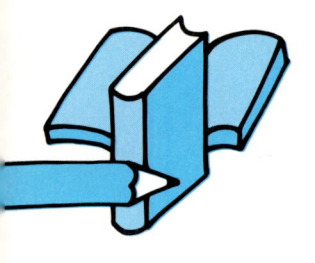

How Did the Writer Feel?

As you read a story carefully, you may be able to understand more than just the words. You may be able to tell how the writer felt when writing the story. Read the sentences below. Think how the writer may have felt about Betsy while writing the story.

Story 1   Betsy is a wonderful girl. She is lots of fun. She smiles at people. Everyone likes her. She is also the best baseball player in our school.

How did the writer feel about Betsy? Write the answer on your paper.

    a. The writer never knew Betsy.
    b. The writer did not like Betsy.
    c. The writer really liked Betsy.

Now read each story on the next page. Think how the writer may have felt while writing the story. Choose an answer that tells how the writer may have felt. Write the answer on your paper.

Story 2 I could look all day at birds flying in the sky. Birds have such beautiful feathers. They make such lovely sounds when they sing and talk to one another. Sometimes I try to sing and talk with birds.

   a. The writer did not really like birds.
   b. The writer knew nothing about birds.
   c. The writer really liked birds.

Story 3 Slugs are ugly creatures. When you touch them, they feel like awful worms. Slugs eat the vegetables in people's gardens. But what would want to eat a slug?

   a. The writer really liked slugs.
   b. The writer wanted slugs for pets.
   c. The writer was disgusted with slugs.

Story 4 Andy always wants to have his own way. He always wants to be first in line. He always wants to win. Now he's broken my new game!

   a. The writer did not know Andy.
   b. The writer was disgusted with Andy.
   c. The writer never thought about Andy.

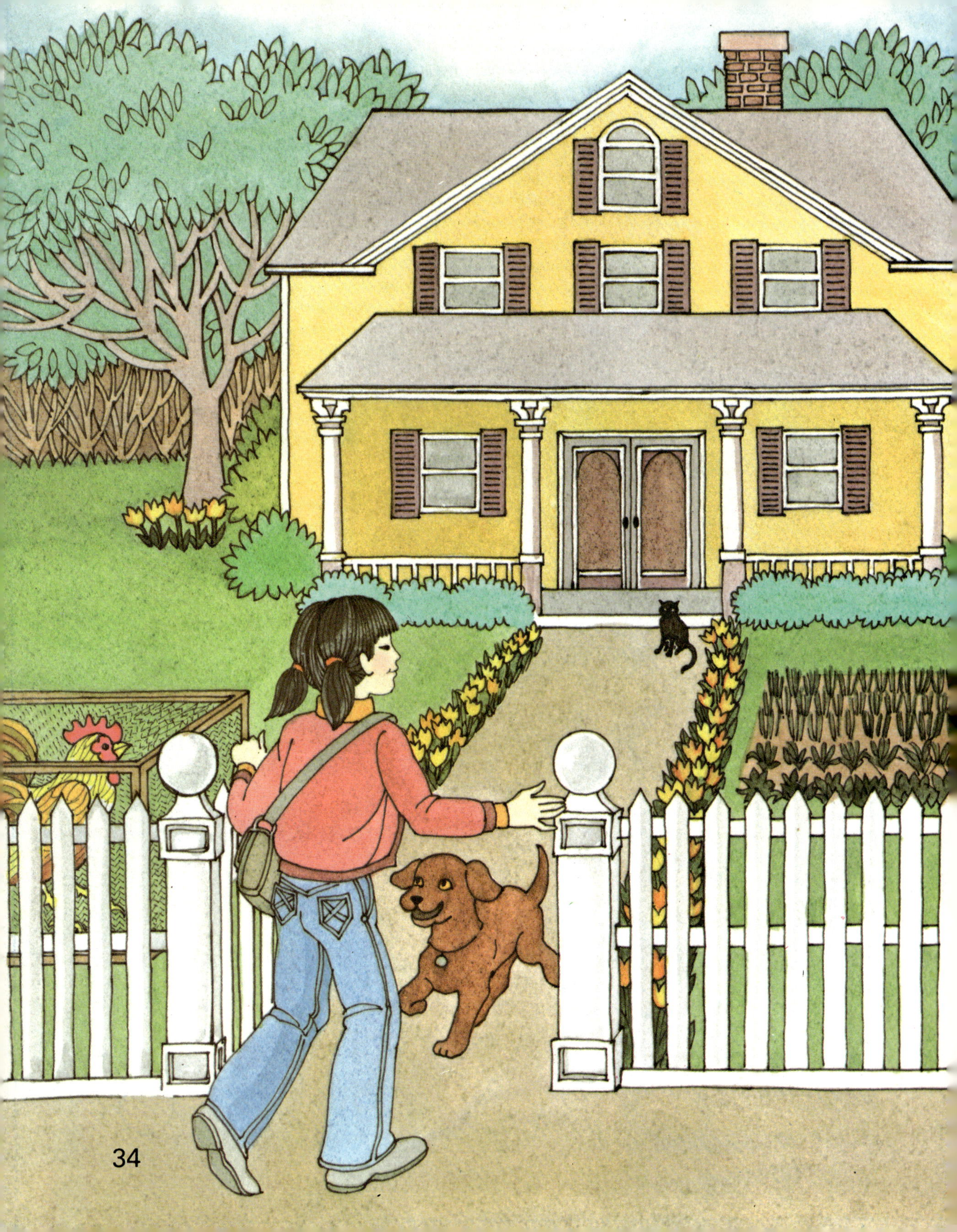

The Rooster Who Understood Japanese

Yoshiko Uchida

Part One

Mr. Lincoln's Crowing

"Mrs. K.!" Miyo called. "I'm here!" Every afternoon when Miyo came home from school, she went to the home of her neighbor, Mrs. Kitamura. Miyo called her "Mrs. K."

Miyo's mother was a doctor and didn't get home until supper time. Sometimes she didn't get home even then. If she didn't, Miyo just stayed on at Mrs. K's.

Mrs. Kitamura was a widow, and she enjoyed Miyo's company. Not that she was lonely. She had a dog named Jefferson, a ten-year-old parrot named Hamilton, a black cat named Leonardo, and a pet rooster named Mr. Lincoln. She talked to all of them in Japanese. She also talked to the onions and potatoes she'd planted in her front yard. She asked them each day to grow plump and delicious.

About the time Miyo came home from school, Mrs. K. was usually outside talking to her potatoes and onions. But today Mrs. K. was nowhere to be seen. She wasn't out front, and she wasn't in back talking to any of her animals either.

Her dog, Jefferson, came to greet Miyo as she opened the gate.

"Hello, Jefferson Kitamura," Miyo said. "Where's Mrs. K.?"

Jefferson wagged his tail and sniffed at Miyo. Then he went back to his special spot at the foot of the willow tree.

Miyo stopped next to see Mr. Lincoln. He was strutting about in his pen. He was making rooster-like sounds and looking very intelligent. Mrs. K. had told Miyo that Mr. Lincoln understood every word she said to him whether she spoke in English or Japanese.

"Mrs. Kitamura, *doko*?" Miyo said, asking Mr. Lincoln where she was.

He cocked his head and looked at her with his small bright eyes. Then he made a squawking sound.

"Maybe Mr. Lincoln does understand Japanese," Miyo thought. "But it certainly doesn't do me any good if I can't understand what he says back to me."

"Never mind," she said aloud. "I'll find her." She hurried toward the house. The back door was open, and Miyo walked in.

"Mrs. K., I'm here!" she called once more.

A high voice repeated, "Mrs. K., I'm here." It was Hamilton, the parrot. He lived in a big gold cage in Mrs. Kitamura's kitchen.

"Hello, Hamilton," Miyo said.

"Hello, Hamilton," he answered back.

Miyo sniffed as she walked through the kitchen. She was hoping she might smell brownies or freshly baked bread. But today there was only the smell of floor wax.

Miyo went through the swinging doors into the dining room. She found Mrs. K. sitting at the big dining-room table. She was doing something Miyo had never seen her do before. She was making herself a cup of ceremonial tea.

Miyo knew what Mrs. K. was doing. She had seen a lady in a pretty kimono perform the Japanese tea ceremony just last month.

Somehow Mrs. K. didn't look quite right. She was preparing the tea in her gardening clothes. She was sitting at a table piled high with old newspapers. She was frowning, too.

Miyo knew the tea ceremony helped to make one feel peaceful and calm.

"Mah!" Mrs. K. said, looking surprised. "I was so busy with my thoughts that I didn't even hear you come in."

Miyo looked at the light, green tea in the tea bowl. She knew it was strong and bitter. "Is that our afternoon tea?" she asked, trying not to look disappointed.

"No, no, not yours," Mrs. K. answered quickly. "Just mine. I make it to calm myself." Then she turned the bowl around carefully and drank it. She drank it in the proper three and a half sips. "There," she sighed.

"Are you calm now?" Miyo asked.

Mrs. K. shook her head. "Not really. As a matter of fact, I am most upset."

Mrs. Kitamura stood up and started toward the kitchen. Usually she was full of fun, but today she hardly smiled at Miyo.

"I've been upset since seven o'clock this morning," she explained suddenly.

"Why?" Miyo asked.

"It's my new neighbor, Mr. Wickett," Mrs. K. said. "He told me that if Mr. Lincoln didn't stop waking him up by crowing at six in the morning, he was going to report me to the police for disturbing the peace! Can you imagine anything so unfriendly?"

Miyo certainly couldn't. "He's mean," she said.

"What am I going to do?" Mrs. K. sighed. "I can't tell Mr. Lincoln he is not to crow anymore. That would be like telling Jefferson not to wag his tail, or telling Leonardo not to groom himself..."

"Or telling Hamilton not to copy us," Miyo said.

"You're right," Mrs. K. agreed. "He is only acting in his natural rooster-like way.

Anyway, everyone should be up by six o'clock."

Miyo wondered what she could say to make Mrs. K. feel better. "I'll ask my mother. She'll know what to do," Miyo said as she left Mrs. Kitamura's house.

Mrs. K. nodded. "I hope so," she said sadly. "In the meantime, I must think of something before six o'clock tomorrow morning."

When Miyo got home, Mother was just starting supper. "Hi, sweetie," she called. "How was Mrs. K.?"

"She was worried," Miyo answered as she began to set the table. "She's got to make Mr. Lincoln stop crowing."

"Whatever for?"

Miyo quickly told Mother about Mr. Wickett. "He's mean," she said, frowning at the thought of him. "Mr. Lincoln doesn't hurt anybody."

But Mother said, "Well, I can see Mr. Wickett's side, too. If I could sleep late, I'm not so sure I'd like having a rooster wake me at six o'clock. Besides," she added, "our town is growing. We're in the city limits now. Maybe Mrs. K. will just have to give Mr. Lincoln away."

Miyo didn't even want to think of such a thing. "But he's not just any old rooster," she said. "Besides," she added, "he doesn't crow very loud."

Mother nodded. "I know," she said. "Well, maybe we can think of something."

But nobody could—not Mother, not Miyo, nor Mrs. K.

Part Two

A Box for Mr. Lincoln

That night Mrs. K. brought Mr. Lincoln inside the house. She put him into a big box in her bedroom.

"Poor Mr. Lincoln," she said to Miyo the next day. "It was hard for him to breathe, and I hardly got any sleep at all. He crowed in the morning anyway. But I don't think Mr. Wickett heard him because so far the police haven't come. But I jump every time my doorbell rings. What on earth are we going to do?"

Miyo wished she had an answer. But all she could say was, "Mama and I are both thinking hard."

Mrs. K. had been so worried she had spent the whole day cooking Japanese food. She thought cooking would take her mind off Mr. Lincoln.

"I made two kinds of *osushi* today," she said to Miyo. She showed Miyo a huge dish of flavored rice rolled in sheets of seaweed. She had also cooked slices of fried beancurd and filled them with rice.

Mrs. K. gave Miyo a dish of *osushi* when she left. "Take some home for supper," she said. "Your mama will be glad not to have to cook tonight."

Miyo felt that neither she nor her mother really deserved the *osushi*. They hadn't come up with one good idea to help Mrs. K.

"I do wish we could think of a way to help Mrs. K.," Mother said as they ate Mrs. K.'s delicious *osushi*.

But Mother was very tired at the end of a long day looking after sick babies and sick children. She just couldn't find any good ideas inside her head. She did say, however, that keeping Mr. Lincoln inside a box in the house was not the answer.

Mrs. K. certainly found out it wasn't. The next night she brought him inside, and Mr. Lincoln poked his way right out of the box. He walked all over her house. He scratched the floors and pecked at her sofa. He got into a fight with Leonardo, the cat. By the time Mrs. K. got to them, there were feathers all over her living room.

"I suppose I will have to give Mr. Lincoln away," Mrs. K. said sadly. "But I can't give him to just anybody. It has to be someone who will love him." Trying to look brave, she said, "If I can't find a new home for Mr. Lincoln, I suppose I will just have to go to jail."

Miyo thought and thought. How in the world could they find just the right person to take Mr. Lincoln? Then, suddenly, she had an idea.

"I know," she said brightly. "I'll put an ad in our class magazine."

Mrs. K. thought about it. "Well," she said slowly, "I suppose it won't do any harm."

What she really meant was that it probably wouldn't do any good either. But Miyo was determined to try. She made her ad very special. She wrote, "WANTED: NICE HOME FOR FRIENDLY, INTELLIGENT ROOSTER. P.S. HE UNDERSTANDS JAPANESE." Then she added, "PLEASE HURRY!"

Her teacher told her it was a fine ad. He suggested that Miyo put in her phone number, too. Miyo also drew a picture of Mr. Lincoln below her ad. She tried to make him look friendly and intelligent.

The magazine came out on Monday. That very afternoon, a police officer rang the doorbell of Mrs. K.'s house.

"I've a complaint, ma'am," he said, "about a rooster?" He seemed to think there might have been some mistake.

Mrs. K. sighed. "Come inside, officer," she said. "I've been expecting you." She supposed now she would just have to go quietly to jail. But first she wanted a cup of tea. "Would you like some tea?" she asked.

Officer McArdle was tired and his feet hurt. "Thank you, ma'am," he said, and he came inside. He looked all around at Mrs. Kitamura's home. It was full of Japanese things he'd never seen. There were Japanese dolls dancing inside glass cases. There were Japanese paintings hanging on the walls. There were Japanese books and newspapers spread out all over the dining room table.

Mrs. K. brought in some tea and cookies. "Now," she said, "please have some tea, officer." She took off her apron and smoothed down her hair. Then she told Officer McArdle all about her troubles with Mr. Lincoln.

He looked understanding, but he said, "You're breaking a city law by having a rooster in your yard. You really should be fined, you know."

"Even if I am only barely inside the city limits?" Mrs. K. asked.

Officer McArdle nodded. "I'm afraid so. I'll give you two more days to get rid of your rooster. Mr. Wickett says you're disturbing the peace."

Then he thanked her for the tea and cookies, and he was gone.

Part Three

Mr. Lincoln's New Home

Miyo was proud of the ad in her class magazine. But no one seemed at all interested in Mr. Lincoln. Instead, a few people told her how much they liked her feature story. It was about Mr. Botts, the school custodian, who was retiring.

She had written, "Say good-by to the best custodian our school ever had. Mr. Botts is retiring. He and Mrs. Botts are going to Far Creek. He is going to eat a lot and sleep a lot and maybe go fishing. So, so long, Mr. Botts. And good luck!"

Her teacher told her it was a fine story.

On her way home, Miyo ran into Mr. Botts himself. He told her it was the first time in his whole life that anyone had written a feature story about him.

When Mr. Botts got home that night, he took off his shoes and sat in his favorite chair. Then he read the magazine from cover to cover. At the bottom of page twenty, he saw Miyo's ad about Mr. Lincoln.

"Tami," he said to Mrs. Botts, who

happened to be Japanese, "how would you like to have a rooster?"

"A what?"

"A rooster," Mr. Botts repeated. "One that understands Japanese."

Mrs. Botts looked at Mr. Botts with wonder in her eyes. Mr. Botts kept right on talking. "When we move to Far Creek," he said, "didn't you say you were going to grow vegetables and raise chickens while I go hunting and fishing?"

Mrs. Botts remembered having said something like that. "Yes, I guess I did."

"Well, if you're going to raise chickens, you'll need a rooster."

"Why, I guess that's so."

"Then we might as well have one that's intelligent and friendly," Mr. Botts said. Then he went right to the telephone to call Miyo.

"I'll take that rooster you want to find a home for," he said. "My wife, Tami, could talk to it in Japanese, too."

Miyo couldn't believe it. Someone had actually read her ad and that someone was Mr. Botts. They would give Mr. Lincoln a fine home. At last, she had done something to help Mrs. K. As soon as she told Mother, she ran right to tell Mrs. K. the good news.

Mrs. K. was just about to stuff Mr. Lincoln into a wooden box for the night. Miyo told her that Mr. Lincoln would have a nice home in Far Creek with Mr. and Mrs. Botts. Mrs. K. gave Miyo such a hug she almost squeezed the breath out of her.

"Hooray! *Banzai!*" Mrs. K. said happily. "Tomorrow we will have a party to celebrate. I shall invite you and your mama and Mr. and Mrs. Botts." Mrs. K. felt so happy, she even decided to invite Mr. Wickett.

"Even though you are a cross person," she said to him, "I suppose you were right. A rooster shouldn't live in a small pen at the edge of town. He should live in the country where nobody will care if he crows at the sun."

Mr. Wickett was a little embarrassed to come to Mrs. K.'s party, but he was too lonely to say no. He came with a box of candy and said, "I'm sorry I gave you so much trouble."

But Mrs. K. told him he shouldn't be sorry. "Life needs a little stirring up now and then," she said. "Besides," she added, "now both Mr. Lincoln and I have found new friends."

Miyo and her mother brought a cake with Mr. Lincoln's name on it. Mr. and Mrs. Botts brought Mrs. K. a plant. "Maybe you can talk to it in Japanese now instead of to Mr. Lincoln," Mrs. Botts said. "And don't worry, I'll take good care of him."

"You come on out to visit us and your rooster any time you like," Mr. Botts added.

Miyo's mother promised that one day soon she would drive them all up to Far Creek. Then they could see how Mr. Lincoln liked his new home.

When the party was over, Mr. Botts carried Mr. Lincoln in a box to the car. Mr. Lincoln gave a squawk of farewell. Mrs. K. promised she would come visit him soon.

"Good-by, Mr. Lincoln. Good-by, Mr. and Mrs. Botts," Miyo called.

From the kitchen, Hamilton, the parrot, screeched. "Good-by, Mr. Lincoln—Good-by."

Jefferson came outside to wag his tail at everybody. Leonardo rubbed up against Mrs. K.'s leg to remind her that he was still there.

Then Mr. Botts honked his horn, and they were gone.

"I hope we'll see each other again soon," Mr. Wickett said to Mrs. K.

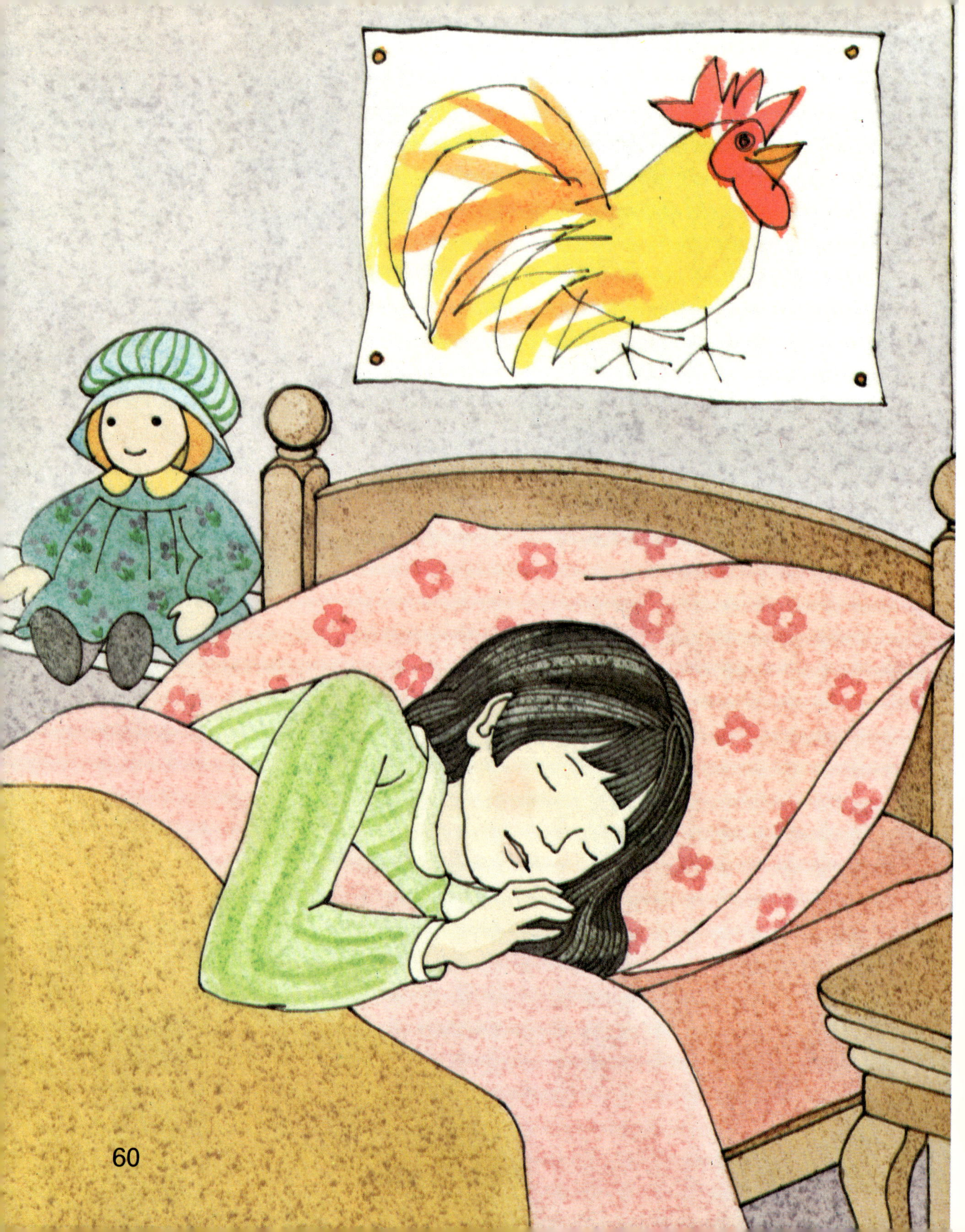

"Good night, Mr. Wickett," she answered. "I'm sure we will."

Miyo and her mother thanked Mrs. K. for the nice party and went home. Mrs. K. would say "good night" to her potatoes and onions before going inside.

"Do you think Mrs. K. will miss Mr. Lincoln a lot?" Miyo asked.

"She will for a while," Mother answered, "but now she has a new friend and neighbor to talk to."

Miyo nodded. That was true. She was glad everything had turned out so well. Miyo went to bed feeling good inside.

"Good night, Mama," she called softly.

"Good night, Miyo," Mother answered.

Then, one by one, the lights went out in all the houses along the street. Soon, only the sounds of insects filled the dark night air.

BUTTERFLY WINGS

How would it be
on a day in June
to open your eyes
in a dark cocoon,

And soften one end
and crawl outside,
and find you had wings
to open wide,

And find you could fly
to a bush or tree
or float on the air
like a boat at sea...

How would it be?

—Aileen Fisher

Hot Enough for You?

Elizabeth Levy

Part One

The Hydrant

Erica lay in her bed. She felt all sticky. She looked at the clock. Seven-thirty.

"Wow," thought Erica. "If it's this hot at seven-thirty in the morning, it's going to be awful by noon." It was the first heat wave of the summer.

Erica got up. Her father was in the kitchen. "Hot enough for you, Erica?" he asked, as he sat down to read the paper.

Before Erica could answer, her older brother Jay came into the room.

"Hot enough for you, Dad?" he asked.

Their father shook his head yes, and kept reading the paper.

Next their mother hurried in, for she was late for work. "Hot enough for everybody?" she asked. She gave Erica and Jay a quick kiss and was gone. Their father left for work a few minutes later.

Erica got her breakfast and looked out the window. Already the street was filled with people. It was too hot to stay inside the apartment. But Erica knew that soon the street would be just as hot.

"Do you want to go outside?" asked Jay.

"I guess so," said Erica. "What do you want to do today?"

"It's too hot to do anything," said Jay. And he was right. It was 95°.

Erica and Jay sat on the steps in front of their apartment. Everyone who went by asked, "Hot enough for you?"

"Nobody ever waits for you to answer," thought Erica. "It's such a silly question, *'Hot enough for you...hot enough for you?'*"

Just then their friend Susan came over. "Hot enough for you?" she asked.

"It's more than hot enough for me!" shouted Erica. "It's much too hot for me."

"I think the heat's got to her," said Jay.

"Let's do something about the heat. Let's not just talk about it," said Erica.

"What?" asked Jay and Susan.

"I don't know," said Erica. "But there has to be something we can do."

Finally, they decided to go for a walk. They got up and walked slowly down the street.

The air seemed to get hotter with every step they took. Finally, Jay stopped. "This is no good," he said. "Walking isn't the way to cool off."

They turned around and walked slowly back toward the apartment. Erica looked down at the sidewalk as she walked. Suddenly she yelled, "Look! There's water!"

"Where?" said Susan.

"In the gutter," said Erica. "I wonder where it's coming from?" She began following the stream of water beside the curb. Jay and Susan followed her.

As they turned the corner, they saw that the water was coming from a fire hydrant. Someone had taken off the cap. Water was pouring out in a hard, steady stream.

"Great!" said Jay. "Now we can cool off!"

They ran to the hydrant. But the water was coming out full blast. The pressure was so strong that it made them fall right off the curb into the gutter.

"Well, at least we're cool," said Erica, picking herself up out of the gutter.

"If only so much water weren't being wasted," sighed Susan.

"The way it is now," said Jay, "you could get hurt trying to play in it."

Erica sat with her toes in the gutter. She stared at the stream of water for a long time.

Part Two
Erica the Inventor

"You know," Erica said at last, "if we could put something with holes in it over the hydrant, the water wouldn't be so strong. We could play in it, and it wouldn't hurt."

"Like what?" asked Susan.

Erica looked around. She couldn't think of anything that would work. Then she saw a top of a garbage can. It was being thrown out. She ran to get it.

"Look," explained Erica, "if we made holes in the garbage can top and somehow got it on the hydrant, it would work!"

"Well," said Jay, "it can't hurt to try."

They got some tools and made holes all over the garbage can top. Then they tried to fit it over the water. But the pressure of the water was so strong that the top kept flying out of their hands.

They were trying it for about the fifth time when a police officer came over and asked, "What's going on here?"

"We didn't open the hydrant," said Jay. "Somebody else did. We just found it open."

"I believe you," said the police officer.

"You're not strong enough to open the hydrant. But what are you doing with that garbage can top?"

"We were trying to make a sprinkler," said Erica. She took the garbage can top and explained to the police officer how it would work.

"You're quite an inventor," said the police officer, as he put the cap back on the hydrant.

"We have to keep these caps on," he said. "The city loses too much water when the hydrants are open. If there were a fire, there might not be enough pressure to put it out. I wish we could have sprinklers though. It's a good way to cool off. Well, stay out of trouble."

He handed the garbage can top back to Erica and went down the street.

The heat wave went on all week. Erica, Susan, and Jay were miserable, as was everyone else in the city.

Then one day, when they were sitting on the steps in front of their apartment, the police officer came by again.

"Where's the inventor?" he asked.

Erica jumped up.

"I've been looking for you," said the police officer. "There's a surprise waiting for you at the police station."

"What kind of surprise?" asked Jay.

"Come with me and you'll see," said the police officer.

At the police station there were lots of people standing around with television cameras.

"I've found her! I've found the inventor!" said the police officer.

Erica looked up and saw a man she knew was the mayor. She couldn't imagine what was going on.

The mayor cleared his throat and began to talk.

"I have something important to say. It's something very nice for all the children of our great city." He stopped and smiled for the television cameras.

"Everyone knows we are having a very bad heat wave," the mayor went on to say. "Some people have opened fire hydrants, but that is very dangerous."

"As of today," said the mayor, "we are going to put sprinkler caps on the hydrants whenever we have a heat wave. The sprinklers will save most of the water, yet the children will still be able to cool off. The little girl who thought up the idea is here beside me. And we are going to put the first sprinkler cap on her block."

Erica was still not sure what was happening.

The mayor and the police officer took her hands. With the cameras following, they walked up the street to the fire hydrant in front of Erica and Jay's house.

"I told your idea to a friend of mine," whispered the police officer. "And my friend took the idea to the mayor. The mayor liked the idea, and now there are going to be sprinklers all over the city."

Then the mayor gave the go-ahead. Two police officers placed a shining new sprinkler cap on the fire hydrant.

"And now," said the mayor, "Erica, the inventor of the fire hydrant sprinkler, her brother, and her friend Susan will show everyone how this wonderful new sprinkler works."

Susan, Jay, and Erica took off their shoes and played in the soft spray. They got all wet and cool.

It looked like so much fun that the mayor decided to take his shoes off and play in the water, too. The police officer did the same thing.

Soon everyone was very wet and very happy, but no one was quite as happy as Erica.

Margarita's Gift

Ann Devendorf

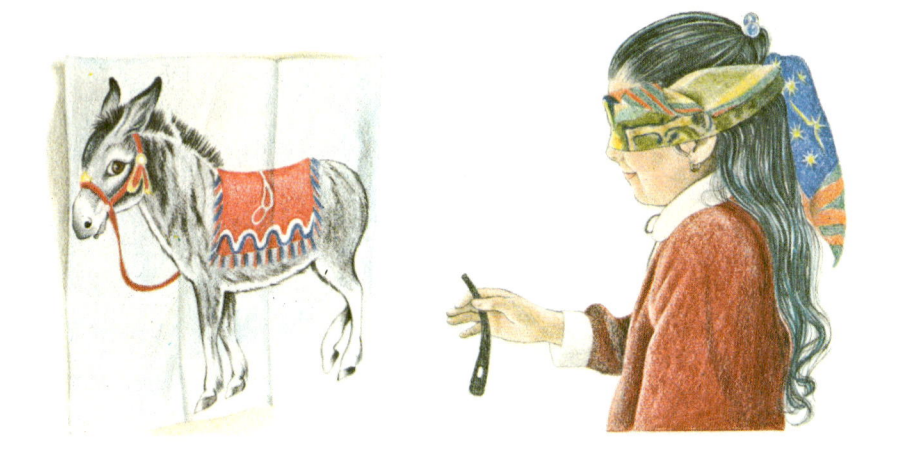

Margarita was at Barbara's birthday party. Margarita felt a little out of place because she didn't speak English very well. She had just moved to the United States from Mexico.

Margarita wasn't very good at the games either. When they played pin-the-tail-on-the-donkey, Margarita pinned the tail right on the tip of one of the donkey's ears! The winner of the game opened her prize. It was a tiny straw horse.

"I bought all the prizes for the party across the border in Mexico," said Barbara to Margarita. "I like to shop in Mexico."

"I do, too," said Margarita. "It's easier for me to shop in Mexico. I speak better Spanish than English."

The next game was guessing the number of beans in a jar. Margarita didn't even come close. She guessed 77, and there were 139 beans in the jar! The winner of the guessing game got six Mexican jumping beans for a prize.

"Hold them in your hand and warm them up," said Barbara to the winner. "Then the beans will begin to jump."

For the last game, they tried to hit a *piñata*. The *piñata* was made in the shape of a horse. It hung on a long rope. The *piñata* could be moved up or down by tugging on the rope.

Margarita knew that the inside of the horse was filled with candies. When the horse was broken, the candies would tumble out.

Margarita watched as each child put on a blindfold and swung at the *piñata* with the handle of a broom. Some of the children hit the horse with glancing blows. Barbara pulled on the rope and made the horse dance away from the swinging broom handle.

Margarita thought, "I know I can hit that *piñata*. I've had practice with *piñatas* many times. I know I must hit above where I last see the horse, because Barbara will pull the horse upward."

Margarita was last. As she was putting on the blindfold, she thought, "I don't want to smash the horse. I know Barbara would like to keep it and hang it in her room."

Margarita brought the broomstick back and swung. She missed. She missed on purpose.

"Oh," sighed Barbara, "I'm so glad my horse isn't smashed." She turned the horse upside down and the candies tumbled from a hole in the top.

Barbara's mother called the children to the table for cake and ice cream. Barbara blew out all the candles on the cake. Margarita enjoyed the cake and ice cream. But she found it difficult to chatter in English with the other children at the table. She felt quite alone.

Then Barbara's mother brought in a huge plate of fortune cookies and put them on the table.

"Oh, good! Fortune cookies!" shouted the children. Their eyes sparkled.

"We got the fortune cookies in Mexico, too," said Barbara.

"I hope I get a good fortune," said one of the children.

"So do I," said another.

Each child carefully picked a fortune cookie from the plate. They cracked them open, and then they groaned.

"The fortunes are written in Spanish!" they exclaimed. "We can't read them!"

"Oh," sighed Barbara. "I never thought about that when I bought them."

"Neither did I," said Barbara's mother. "I should have realized the fortunes would be written in Spanish!"

"I'm so disappointed," said Barbara.

"Don't be," said Margarita. "I can read the fortunes. I'll be happy to do so."

"Read mine!" called a child.

"And mine, too!" called another.

All the children crowded around Margarita. She read their fortunes and translated them into English. The children laughed and giggled. Margarita did, too.

"I'm so glad you can read Spanish," said Barbara.

"We all are," the children agreed.

Margarita felt happy inside. She peeked again at her fortune. It read: "*Su futuro sera muy contento.*" This means, "Your future will be very happy."

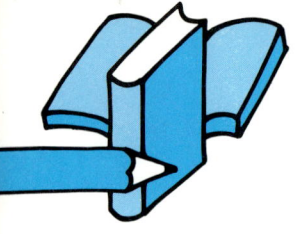

What's the Meaning of This?

Some words look alike and sound alike. But they have different meanings. You have to read how the word is used in a sentence. Then you can find out what it means.

> I went to the bank to get some money.
> We often sit on the bank of the river.

In the first sentence, *bank* means "a place where people keep their money." In the second sentence, *bank* means "the land on the side of a river or stream."

Read each set of meanings. Then read the numbered sentences. Choose the right meaning for each sentence. Then write that meaning on your paper.

Set A
To play is to have fun.
A play is a story that people act out.

1. We're doing a play about Abe Lincoln.
    1. A play is a story that people act out.

2. Gordon wants to play all day.
3. The play will begin at seven o'clock.

Set B

A ring is the sound of a bell.
A ring is a band someone wears on a finger.

1. I lost my ring in the ocean.
2. We heard the ring of a bell.

Set C

A watch is a small timepiece that is often worn on the arm.
To watch is to look at something closely and carefully.

1. Allison broke her watch while playing.
2. Please watch the baby until I get back.

Set D

A tip is the end of something.
A tip is money given to someone for doing a job well.

1. We left a large tip in the restaurant after a fine meal.
2. The tip of the mountain was in a cloud.

Harlequin
and The Gift of Many Colors

Adapted from a story by Remy Charlip and Burton Supree

Paintings by Remy Charlip

Part One
Only a Blanket

Harlequin awoke. His room was dark. The stars and the moon were still in the sky. It was chilly when he got out of bed, so Harlequin wrapped his blanket around him. When he walked to the window, he felt as if he were wearing the night.

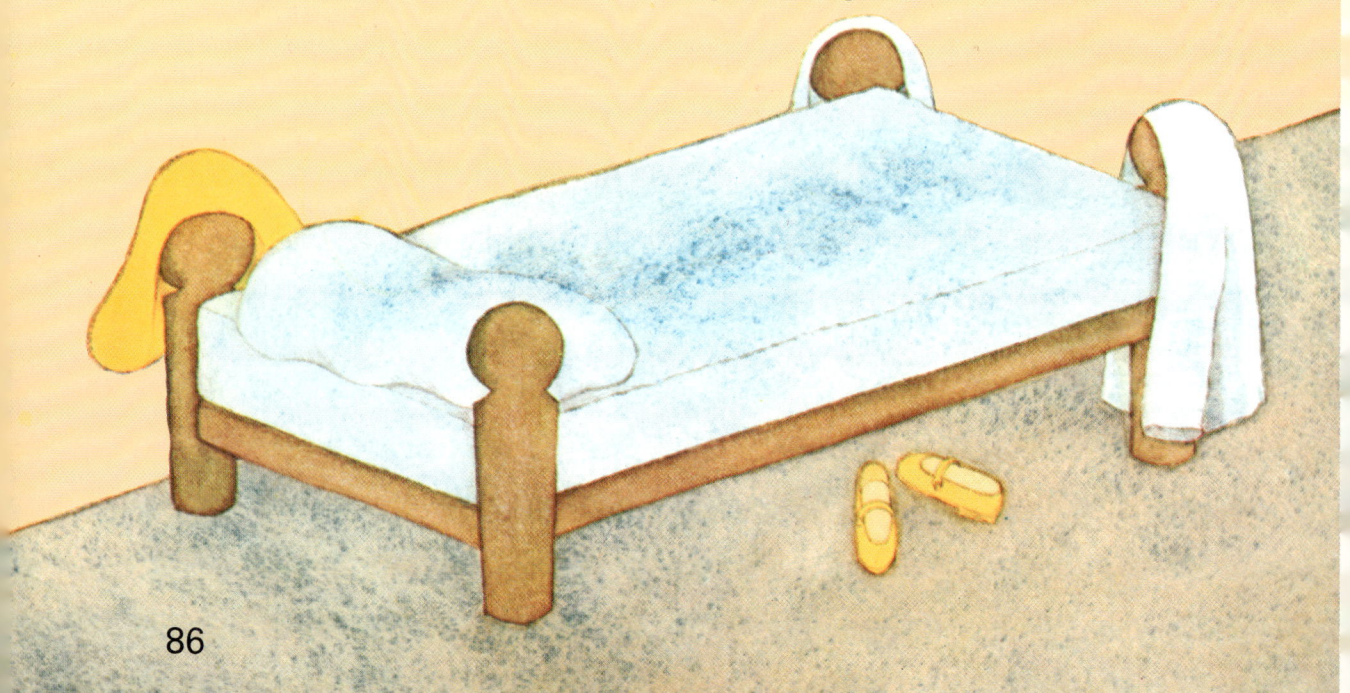

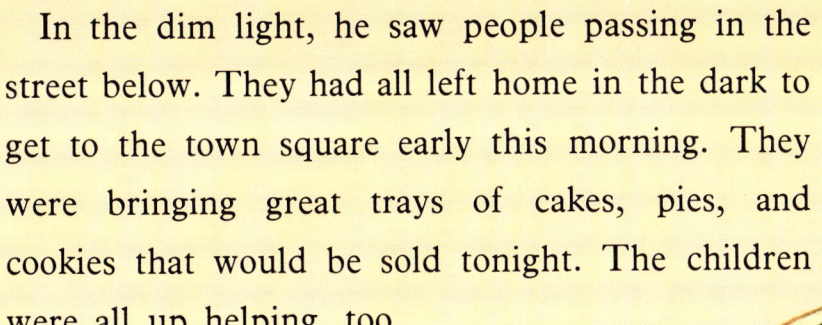

In the dim light, he saw people passing in the street below. They had all left home in the dark to get to the town square early this morning. They were bringing great trays of cakes, pies, and cookies that would be sold tonight. The children were all up helping, too.

But Harlequin sighed. He got back into his warm bed. He pulled the covers over his head.

The children could hardly wait for tonight's great Carnival. There would be games with prizes and candy and ice cream. And there would be dancing and singing and joking with all their friends.

"But where is Harlequin?" one of the children asked, "I haven't seen him all morning."

Harlequin was almost always the first one up, and the one to lead the others in all sorts of fun.

"Maybe he was bad and his mother won't let him come out."

"Maybe he's sick. We'd better go see." And they all ran off to Harlequin's house.

"Harlequin! Harlequin, are you there?" He appeared at the window wearing his blanket.

"Are you all right? Come on out!" His friends all started talking at once.

"Harlequin, the fireworks are all finished."

"My father says I can stay up as late as I want."

"Can you smell the chocolate?"

"Hurry, let's get back to the square."

Slowly Harlequin dressed and came down.

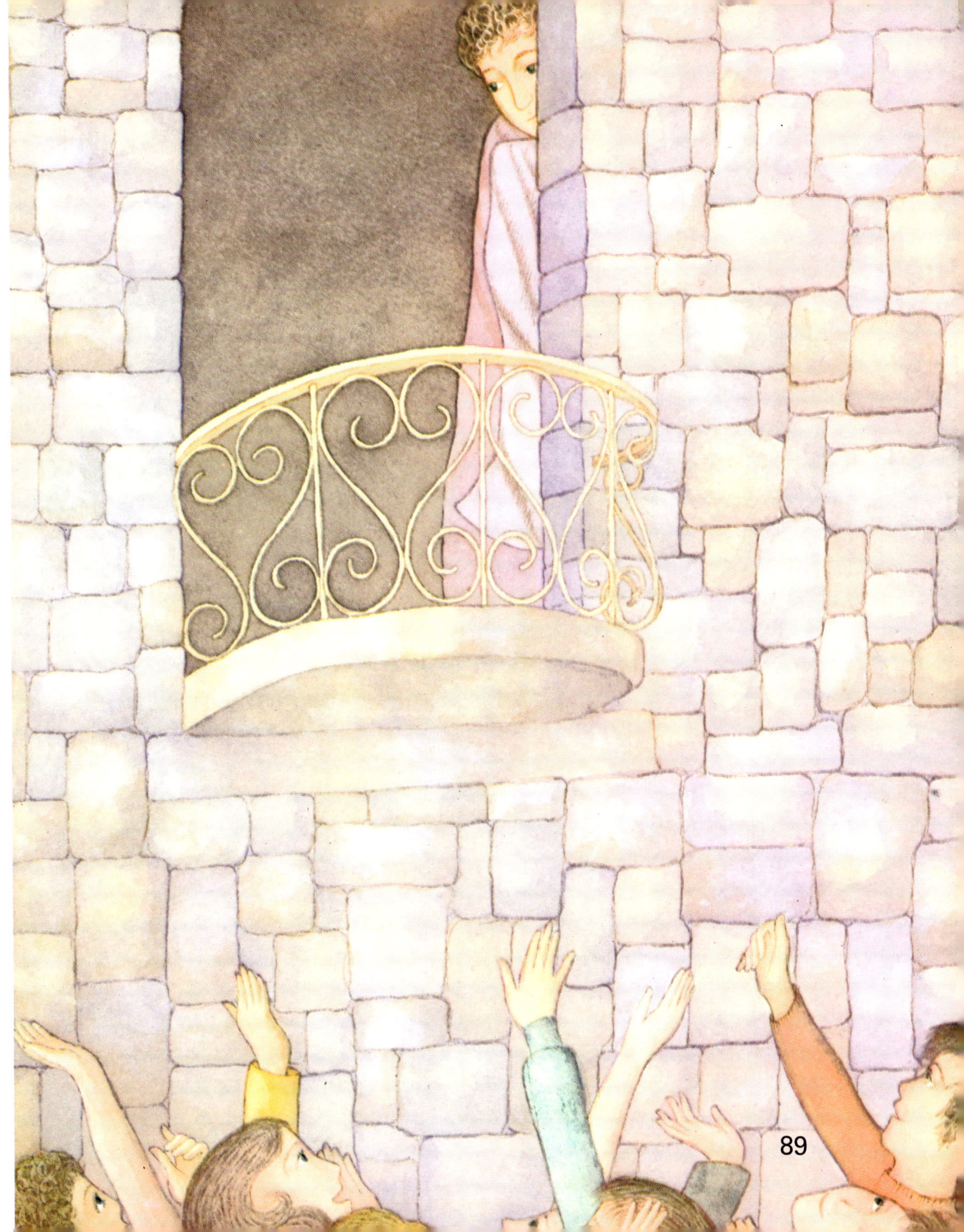

Walking back to the square, the children began to talk about the best thing of all. Tonight everyone was going to wear a new costume for the first time. With masks over their faces no one would know them. Oh, what tricks they would get away with then!

But it was hard not to brag and tease with little hints about their costumes.

"Mine is yellow."

"My suit is soft and blue."

"Wait till you see mine. It's the most beautiful red."

"I've got the biggest green buttons you ever saw." They were all talking at once, parading around in their old clothes, and showing off as if they were already wearing their new ones.

It was only then that they noticed how quiet and gloomy Harlequin had been all this time.

"What are you going to wear tonight, Harlequin?" They all turned to him.

Harlequin didn't say anything.

"Oh, Harlequin, you've got to tell. We told you."

"Well," said Harlequin, thinking fast, "I'll wear my blanket as a cape."

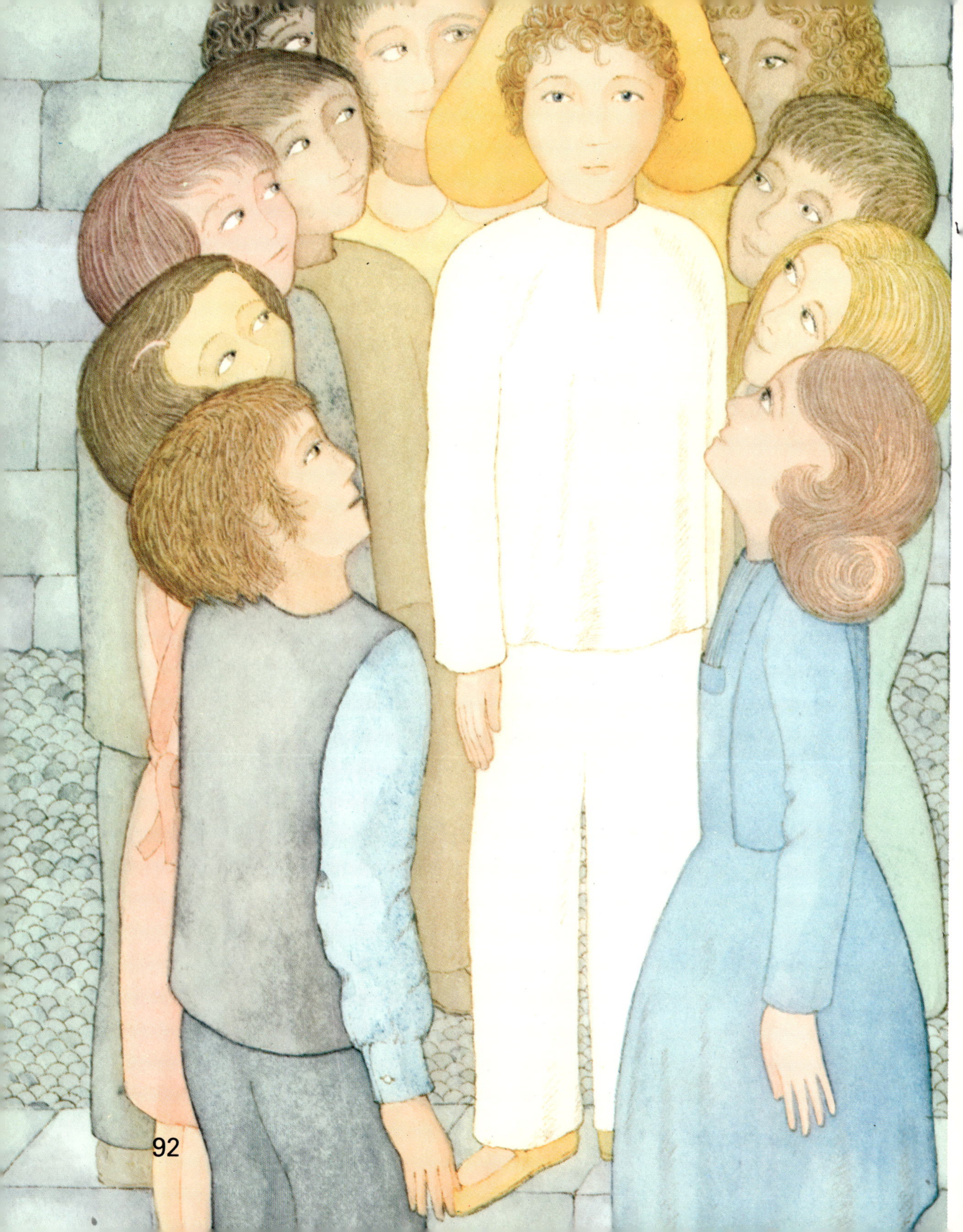

They thought Harlequin was fooling them as he often did.

"Not that old thing!"

"Come on, Harlequin, give us a clue."

"What color is it?"

"What are you going to wear tonight?"

"Nothing," Harlequin answered. "I'm not even coming tonight."

And he turned and ran away.

Harlequin not coming? How could that be? How could he miss Carnival?

Perhaps he was still fooling. He was always playing tricks.

"Wait," one of them said, "I think I know why he's not coming tonight. He doesn't have a new costume."

And it was then that they all understood what was the matter. Harlequin had nothing to wear because his mother was too poor to buy him a costume.

"What can we do? Where can we get him a costume?" they said.

Part Two
A Piece of Cloth

"I know! I have an idea. My coat doesn't need to be so long. I can cut some off and give it to Harlequin. And if we each give him a piece of cloth, then he will have enough for a whole new costume."

"That's true! My dress doesn't need to be so long either."

"Let's go and get our cloth and meet in front of Harlequin's house."

The sun was high when all the children met at Harlequin's house. Each one was carrying a piece of cloth.

When Harlequin answered the knock on the door, he was surprised to see all his friends. Then they held out the pieces of cloth and happily pushed them into his hands.

But when the children saw Harlequin's arms filled with the cut-off bits and scraps, they were sad. Each piece was a different shape and size and color. Some were shiny, some were fuzzy. None of the pieces matched. They looked like a bunch of old rags.

95

Harlequin smiled and thanked them. But the children were afraid they had made him more unhappy by giving him such a useless gift.

"I feel so stupid," one of them whispered.

Unhappily they said good-by and left.

When they were gone, Harlequin stared at the scraps of cloth in his arms.

"What can I do with these?" he thought. "Nothing. Not one piece is big enough for a pant leg or even a sleeve."

He climbed the stairs to his room, thinking that he would not go out again until Carnival was over.

He threw the pieces of cloth into the air. But as the pieces fell to the floor, one piece stuck to his shirt. He looked at it for a moment. And then he had an idea.

When his mother came home, Harlequin told her all that had happened.

Then he told her his idea.

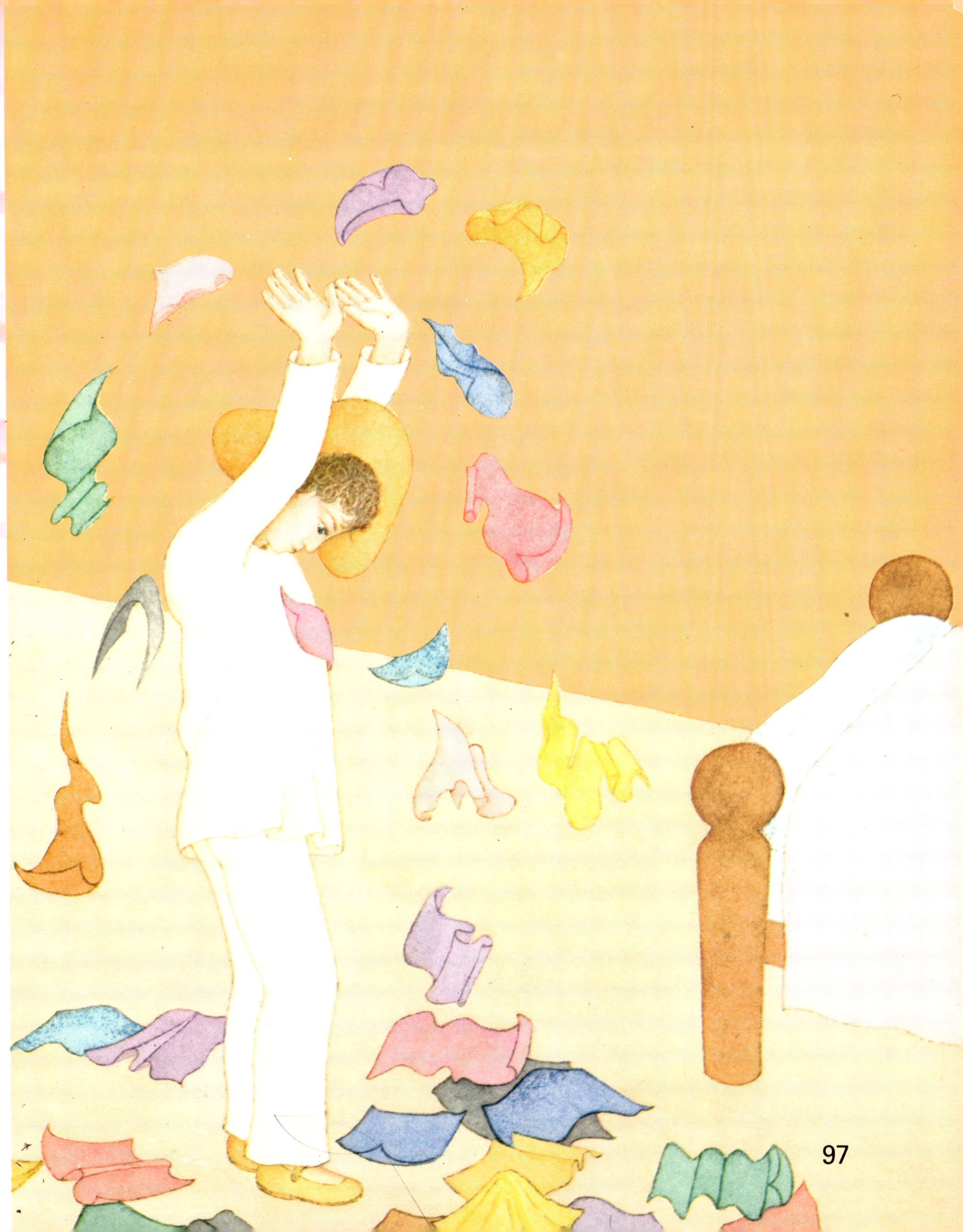

"Do you think if we put all these scraps onto my old suit, it would make a good costume?"

His mother looked at the pieces of cloth. She turned them over and over in her hands. Would it work?

Then she smiled, "I think it would be beautiful."

And they both set to work. Harlequin chose a blue piece. Then he pinned a green one next to it. He pinned all the pieces where he wanted them. His mother began to sew them on.

The sewing took a long time. While his mother was sewing the pieces on his old pants, Harlequin climbed into bed to keep warm. And before he knew it, he had fallen asleep.

But his mother worked on, worried that she might not be able to finish in time.

"Wake up, Harlequin, it's all finished!"

Moonlight streamed into his room. He heard music and shouting far away. He blinked his eyes. For a moment he didn't know where he was.

Then he knew that he was not dreaming. His mother was standing by his bed, smiling. She was holding up a beautiful rainbow-colored suit.

"It's finished!" He threw the covers off and jumped out of bed. "Let me put it on!"

"How wonderful you look!" his mother said proudly. He spun around and around, as bright as a butterfly. "Oh, thank you, I love it," Harlequin said as he put on his mask and his big hat. "It's wonderful!"

And in a moment he ran off to the town square.

The town square was wild with color and noise. All the world seemed to be dancing and singing there. Wonderful smells of cooking meats and sweet pies filled the air. Musicians were playing all the songs everyone liked to hear.

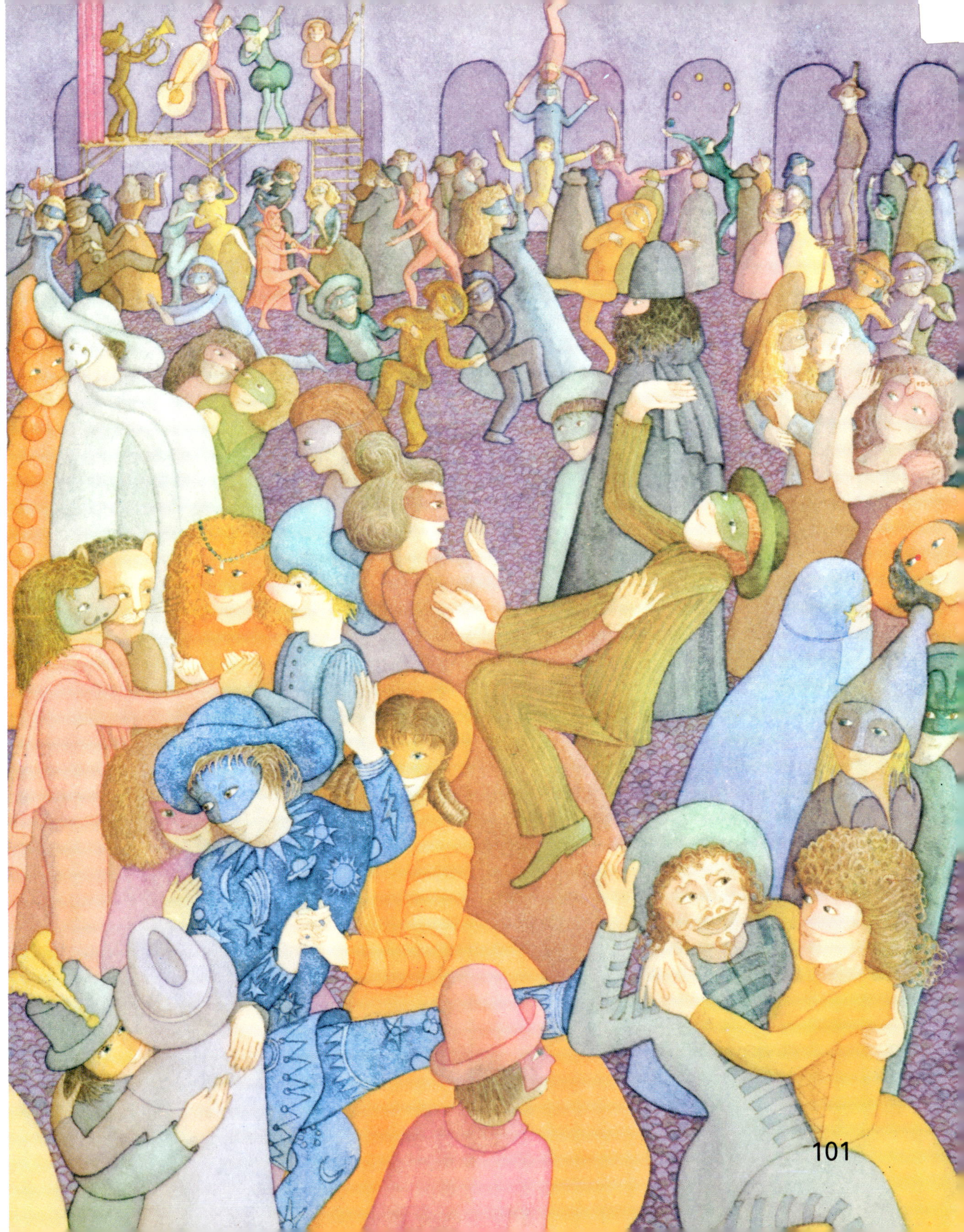

Harlequin's friends had all come early because the first one to come to a booth to buy something did not have to pay. They laughed and joked as they ran from one booth to another, trying to guess who was behind each mask. But they kept looking out for Harlequin, too. They were hoping that by some chance their best friend might be able to come to Carnival.

Suddenly someone appeared in a costume so fantastic that everyone stopped what they were doing. The children all gathered around to see.

"What a splendid costume!"

"I've never seen anything so beautiful!"

"Who is it?"

"Where is he from?"

"Do you know him?" No one knew.

Whoever it was, he began to leap and dance and turn so joyfully that the crowd laughed and clapped with joy. All the many different colors he wore sparkled in the light.

In a flash one of the children noticed a piece of his own costume.

"That piece of blue is mine!" he shouted.

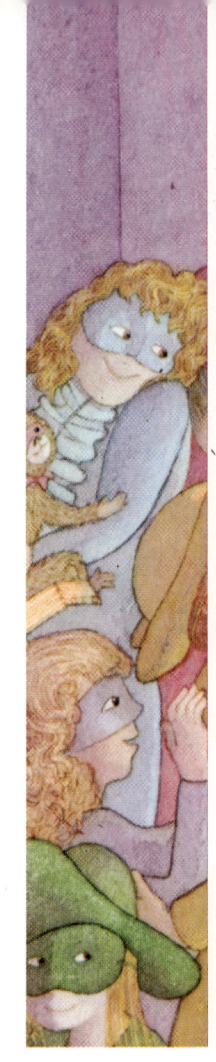

"That shiny red piece is mine!" said another. "That must be Harlequin!"

"Harlequin! Harlequin!" the children cheered, as they raced through the crowd. They danced around, hugging him and each other.

And Harlequin was the happiest of them all on this happy night, for he was clothed in the love of his friends.

Museum of Modern Art, Paris
European Art Color Slides

    This painting of Harlequin was done in 1923. It was painted by a very famous artist named Pablo Picasso. Throughout his lifetime Picasso painted many different Harlequins.

Picasso

Nancy White

Part One
His Younger Years

When Pablo Picasso was a little boy, he lived in a little town in Spain. Nobody ever asked him what he wanted to be when he grew up. Everybody knew that he was already an artist.

His mother liked to tell people that his first words were, "Piz, piz!" This is baby talk for *lápiz,* which is the Spanish word for *pencil.* Stretched out on the floor with a piece of paper and his pencil, Pablo drew pictures even before he had learned to walk. As a very little boy, he liked crayons and chalk better than any of his other toys.

Pablo's father, Don José, was an artist. He was very proud of his son. He spent a lot of time teaching the little boy how to draw and paint. Pablo's ability delighted all of his family and their friends.

Using only one line, he could draw a person, an animal, or a bird that looked almost alive. He often played the "Animal Game" with his little sister Lola and his young friends. His big eyes sparkling, he would say to them, "Do you want a little horse? Or a dog? Or a bull?" Then he would quickly cut out a tiny paper animal that was shaped just like a dog, or a horse, or a bull.

Pablo did not like school. All he really wanted to do was draw. He spent many happy hours in his father's studio. He drew pictures of pigeons he saw through the windows. He made many drawings of Lola. He never grew tired of watching his father work or listening to him explain the uses of pencils and chalk and different kinds of paint.

When Pablo was ten years old, things suddenly changed. Don José took a job as an art teacher and Pablo went to his father's school. Besides teaching, Don José painted pictures to be sold. After school he often asked Pablo to help with these paintings. One day Don José went for a walk, leaving Pablo to finish a painting of some pigeons. When he returned, he stood for a long time looking at the finished picture. Pablo waited, watching his father's face.

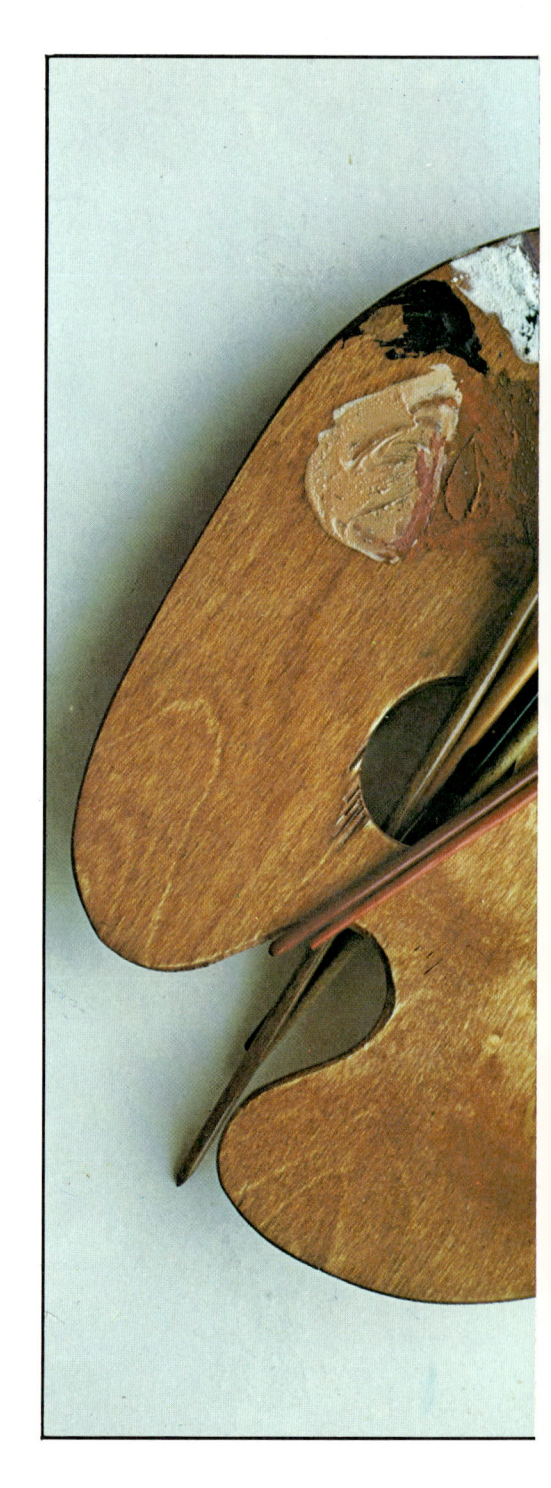

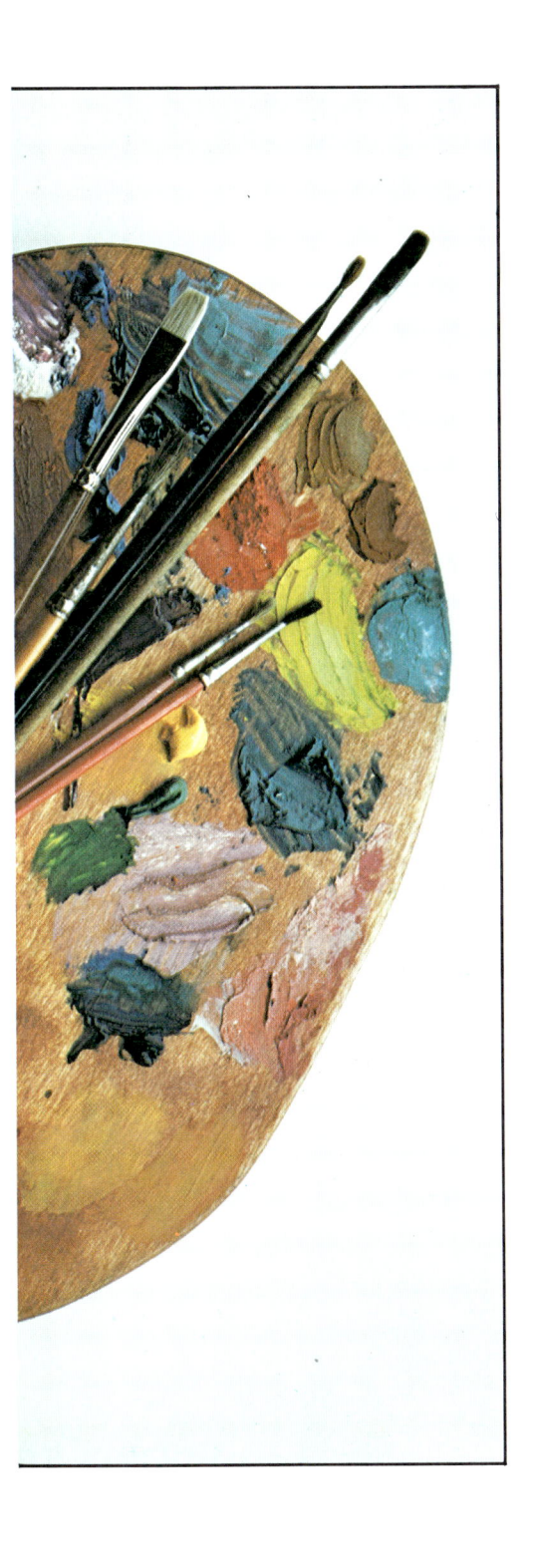

It was very quiet in the studio. Finally, Don José walked over to his work table. He began gathering up his brushes and paint. He put everything in a big box. Then he handed the box to Pablo.

He told Pablo that from now on there would be only one artist in the family. The pigeons in the picture were so real that it seemed as though they might fly away. Don José now knew that Pablo's ability was far greater than his own. He himself would give up painting and spend his time teaching his son.

When Pablo was fourteen, the family moved to Barcelona. Don José began teaching at the School of Fine Arts. Pablo was excited about living in a big city and being near the art school.

Because of Don José, the school decided to let Pablo take the test for the best class. For this test, each artist was given four weeks to finish a drawing. Pablo finished his in one day. And his work was so good that he joined the class at once. During the rest of his life, Pablo kept this ability to work quickly. Some of his best pictures were painted in a very short time.

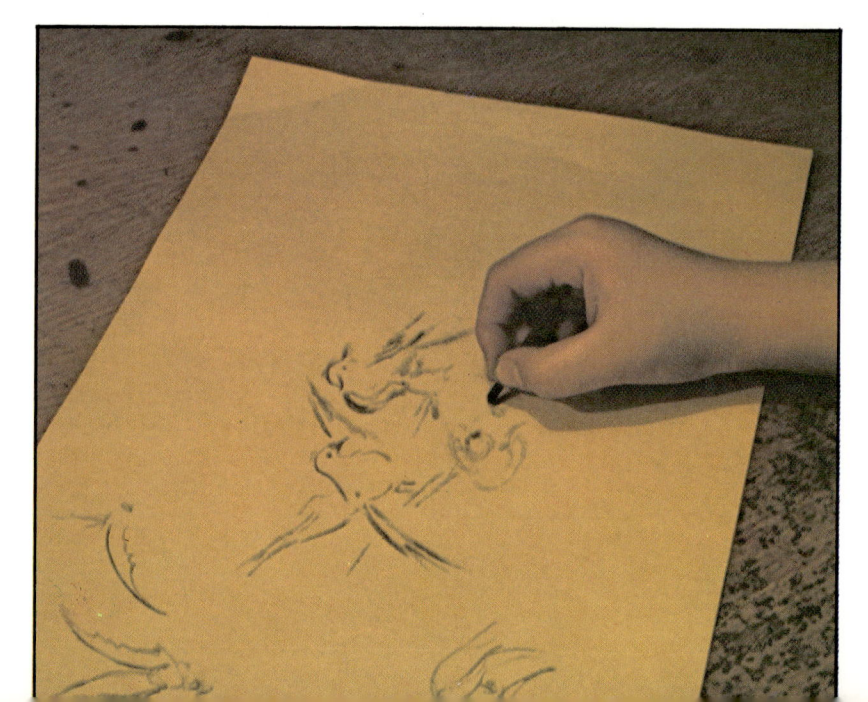

Part Two
A Very Famous Artist

When Pablo was sixteen, he went to Madrid to study art. But he became very sick and had to leave school. He spent the summer at the home of a friend in the country. Here Pablo had fields, farm animals, and new people to draw.

Returning to Barcelona the following fall, Pablo saw that he would have to make some money by painting and selling some pictures.

Some of Pablo's pictures won prizes. But people wouldn't buy them when they found out the artist was a teenager.

When he was nineteen years old, Pablo decided that he must go to Paris, where he could be with other young artists and writers. In Paris his money did not last very long, and Pablo did not sell many of his pictures.

During these years he was often cold, hungry, and sad. But he kept on painting and painting and painting. The people he saw along the waterfront and on the streets were cold, hungry, and sad, too. He watched them. Then he went home to his tiny studio and painted them. He tried to remember just how they looked, and how they made him feel. These years have become known as his "Blue Period."

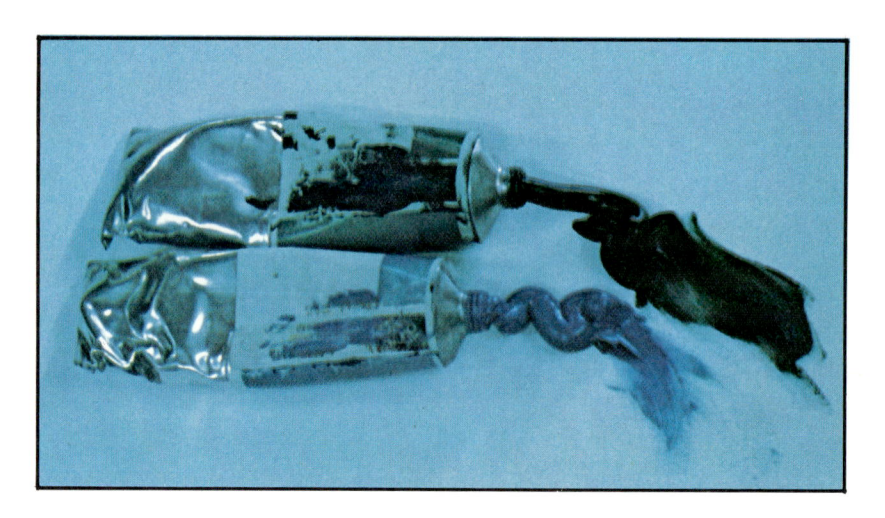

During this period, the colors of his pictures were mostly blues, greens, and grays. These colors reflected his sadness and the sadness of the people he painted.

This picture of Harlequin was painted during Picasso's "Blue Period."

113

Baltimore Museum of Art, Francis B. Mayer

    At the age of twenty-three, Picasso moved to Paris for good. At last people began to want his pictures. The next few years are called his "Rose Period." During this period, he painted in happy colors: pinks and reds. This picture was painted during Picasso's "Rose Period."

Picasso later started a type of painting which he thought was more important than anything he had ever done. It is called "Cubism." This picture is a cubist painting.

Pablo Picasso, whose art is loved throughout the world, was one of the most famous artists of all time.

Walter In Love

Alicen White

Walter was in love.

Walter was in love with Tita.

Tita was a beautiful dancer from Spain. She was a Spanish cocker spaniel, proud as well as pretty.

Walter was not proud, but he was handsome. He was an American cocker spaniel.

He was a dog-about-town.

Walter was a happy dog until he saw Tita. Then he got to be moony. He fell madly in love with her. He went to the theater to look at Tita every night for sixty-six nights. Also Wednesday and Saturday afternoons.

He sent her boxes of roses—red roses and white roses, yellow roses and pink roses. He sent her boxes of candy—hard candy and soft candy, coffee candy and peppermint candy. He sent her boxes of beads—gold beads and silver beads, small and large.

He sat by the stage door each night to see Tita come out after the show. He wore his best top hat, white tie, and black tails, of course. But every night she walked past him with her nose in the air, decked out in the beads he had sent her. She had a rose between her teeth, and a box of candy in her paws. She did not know it was Walter who was sending her all these fine things.

You see, Walter was not good at writing. He wrote all the letters backwards. So, of course, he wrote WALTER for "Walter." Tita did not understand this. She could not read the name of her admirer. If you had been Tita, you would have guessed it. But remember, she left school when she was only two. Tita always got the roses and the candy and the beads, because the card on each box was always right. 'TO TITA' it said.

Walter could not write 'TO TITA' the wrong way, because the letters are the same backwards and forwards. Turned around they still spell 'TO TITA.' Lucky for Tita!

Well, time went by, and still Tita did not know that Walter loved her. He was too shy to speak to her. All his pocket money went for roses and candy and beads for Tita. He could not eat his dinner. At night, because he could not sleep, he would stare up at the moon. Then he would feel moonier than ever. Walter was so miserable that he made up his mind to write Tita a letter.

He got some lovely paper at the best store in town. He bought a pen with a long feather on it, and this is what he wrote:

DEAREST TITA,
I LOVE YOU DEEPLY.
I ADORE THE STARS YOU
GAZE ON. I BEG YOU SMILE
TONIGHT AS YOU PASS ME BY.
PLEASE BE KIND.
I KISS YOUR LITTLE PAWS.
I'D DIE FOR YOU.
SORRY YOURSELESSLY YOURS,
WALTER P. BARKER

That night Walter did not send Tita roses or candy or beads. Just the letter. Then he sat shyly in his usual spot outside the theater and hoped.

Tita found the letter on her dressing table after the last dance number. She tore it open but could not read it.

"Is it in French?" she asked her French maid.

"No, madame. It is a Chinese fan letter," said the maid.

"But I do not understand Chinese," said Tita. "So pin it up on the wall beside my Japanese fan letter."

Then she turned her back to the dressing table, took up her looking glass, and began to comb her lovely long ears.

But what did she see reflected in her little mirror through the big one over the dressing table? Walter's letter!

Now it did not look so much like a Chinese fan letter. Tita could read two words in English—'YOU' and 'I'—as well as 'TITA,' of course.

"It is a code and I am going to crack it!" cried Tita, throwing down her comb. She tore Walter's letter down from the wall. Her pretty nose sniffed each word in turn. At the ninth word, 'THƎ,' she stopped and gave a sharp yell.

"That's it! 'THƎ' means 'THE.' It is a well-known English word. How clever I am! The 'E' is turned the wrong way, and so are the other letters. I'll turn them all the right way at once!"

Using her lipstick as a pencil, Tita wrote Walter's letter the right way round on the big dressing table mirror.

This is what it said:

DEAREST TITA,
I LOVE YOU DEEPLY.
I ADORE THE STAGE YOU DANCE ON.
I BEG ONE SMILE TONIGHT AS YOU PASS ME BY.
PLEASE BE KIND.
I KISS YOUR LITTLE PAWS.
I'D DIE FOR YOU.
SLEEPLESSLY YOURS,
WALTER P. BARKER

"Walter! The admirer who sends me boxes and boxes of roses and candy and beads," cried Tita, sticking a red rose behind her ear. "He must be the handsome dog who sits outside in the cold each night to see me step into my car!"

"He must be very rich, madame," sighed Mimi, the French maid.

"I like that," said Tita. "And I like it that he is kind and good and would die for me."

"Maybe," said Mimi.

"I am sure of it!" cried Tita. "I must not keep him waiting one more night."

When she walked out of the stage door, there sat Walter as usual. His eyes were shining full of love.

Then Tita smiled. Her smile lit up the sky for Walter, like the sun and the moon and all the stars.

"Will you marry me, my love?" he asked, softly holding her feathery paw in his.

"I am yours!" whispered the beautiful Spanish spaniel, her face close to his.

Together they walked off to Walter's big car. Walter was a happy dog again. But Tita never told him how near he had come to losing her because of his back-to-front paw-writing.

So he wrote love notes to her that way, quite happily, for the rest of their lives.

Don't tell me that I talk too much!

Don't tell me that I talk too much!
Don't say it!
Don't you dare!
I only say important things
Like why it's raining where.
Or when or how or why or what
Might happen here or there.
And why a thing is this or that
And who is bound to care.
So don't tell me I talk too much!
Don't say it!
DON'T YOU DARE!

—*Arnold Spilka*

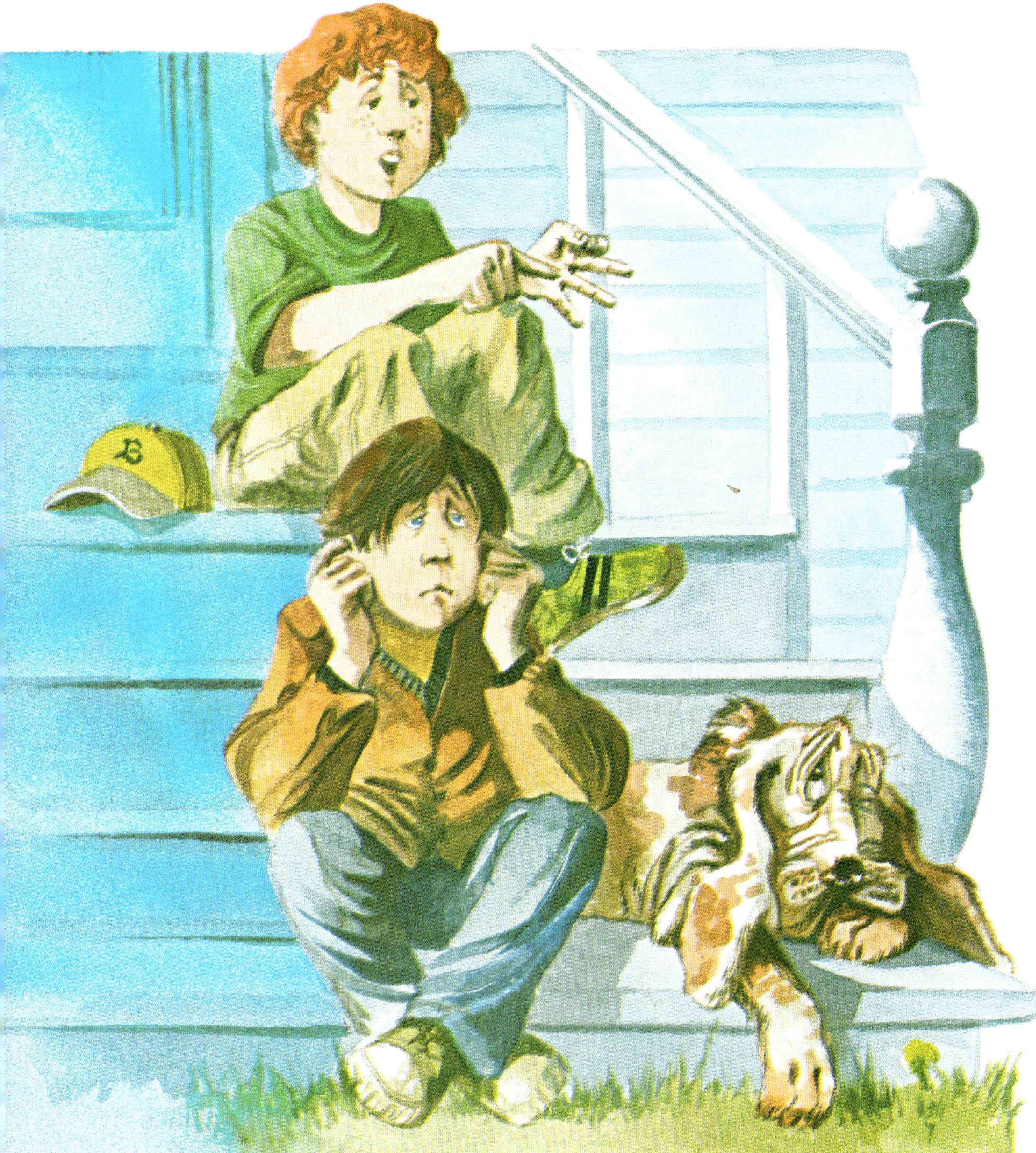

THE FRIENDSHIP GAME

Dina Anastasio

The first day in any new school is hard. But the first day in a new school where everyone speaks French and you speak English is awful! Just ask Jennifer!

Of course, Mademoiselle Sagan, the third-grade teacher, spoke French *and* English. But no one else did. No one but Jennifer. She spoke a little French.

She could say: *Good morning, Good night, Give me some ice cream, please, Where is the ladies' room?* and a few other things. But she didn't know enough to strike up a friendship with anyone in her class who didn't speak English at all.

Jennifer didn't make any friends. She didn't even make an enemy! No one seemed to know that Jennifer was even there. And, before long, she began to feel a bit like an old shoe.

When her father had first told her about his new job and moving to Paris, Jennifer had been quite excited. And when they had talked about schools, she thought it would be exciting to go to a French school. She would meet new people and she would learn to speak French much faster.

It had all sounded so perfect then. But somehow it hadn't turned out that way. Here she was in a French school, with French children, and no one to talk to.

Since Jennifer was not a quitter, she tried very hard to make the best of it. The other kids weren't really mean to her or anything. They just acted like she wasn't there.

Jennifer sat in the very back of the room. She never said anything in class, since everyone was speaking French. So you can see why everyone forgot that she was there.

That evening her father said, "Well, Jennifer, you'll just have to learn to speak French right away." And her mother said, "That's right, dear. The other children aren't going to learn English, so you'll just have to try harder to learn French."

So Jennifer tried harder. She learned to say: *Do you have any hot dogs?* and *Boy, is it hot in here!* and *The rocket crash-landed!* and a few other things. But her life didn't get any easier. She still didn't make any friends.

The loneliest time of Jennifer's day was always recess. The other children played games that she didn't know. They would have been easy enough to learn had Jennifer known how to speak French. But since she didn't, she had to spend each recess alone for a long time.

One day, the other children were playing a game that looked something like tag. Jennifer went inside and asked Mademoiselle Sagan for a piece of chalk. With it she drew a hopscotch game on the sidewalk and started to play by herself. It was no fun alone, so she pretended that she was playing with a friend. This way she had someone to play with, and yet she always won the game. For the first time in a long time, Jennifer began to have a little fun.

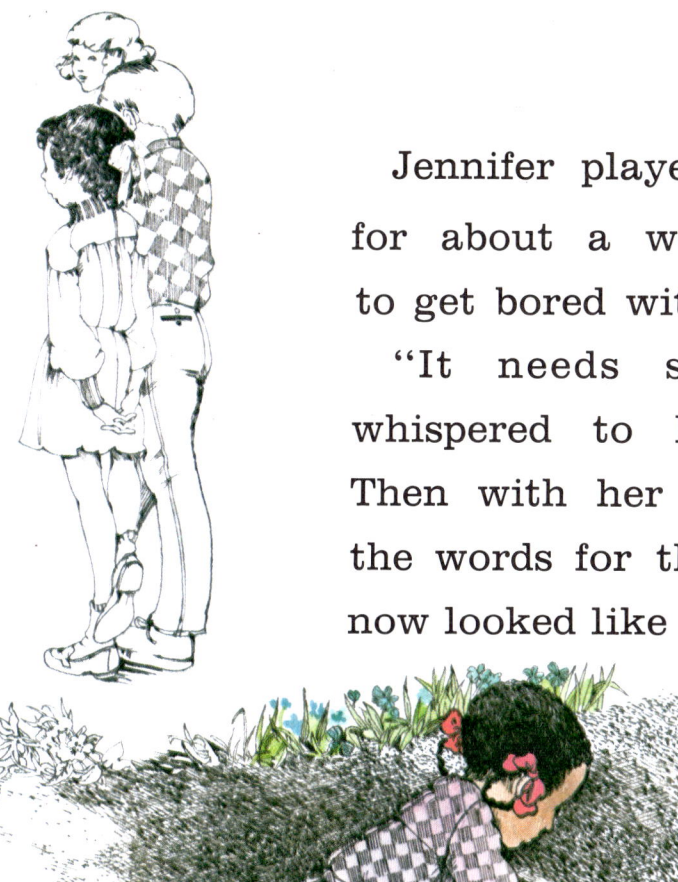

Jennifer played hopscotch at recess for about a week before she began to get bored with it.

"It needs something!" Jennifer whispered to her imaginary friend. Then with her chalk, she wrote out the words for the numbers. The game now looked like this:

It wasn't very different, but it made her feel a little more at home.

Whenever Jennifer and her imaginary friend played hopscotch, they said the numbers out loud as they jumped. Life was beginning to look a lot better for Jennifer.

Then one day, Jennifer noticed that a girl in her class was watching her. Her name was Mimi. All of the other girls seemed to like her very much.

"She must think we're crazy," Jennifer whispered to her imaginary friend. And she quickly stopped counting.

The next day, when Jennifer was playing, Mimi walked over and watched her very carefully.

Jennifer said "hello" in French, and Mimi said the same. But they didn't say anything else. *The rocket crash-landed!* or *Where is the ladies' room?* would have sounded pretty silly. Jennifer still didn't know how to say, *Do you want to play?* or *Nice day, isn't it?* or anything like that. And so they just stood there, smiling at each other. Jennifer felt very foolish.

Suddenly Mimi leaned down. She picked up the piece of chalk and began to write on Jennifer's hopscotch game. When she was through, the game looked like this:

Then Mimi picked up a stone, threw it on the number "one," and began to play. As she jumped, she pronounced the French numbers that she had written, very carefully. When she was done, she pointed to the game and said "you go," in English.

Jennifer threw her stone on "one" and began to hop. As she hopped onto each square, she said the number in French.

When she was finished, Mimi cried "oui, oui," (which is French for *yes, yes*). Jennifer began to play again, but this time she said the numbers in English as she jumped. She was very careful in pronouncing them very clearly.

Next Mimi played, saying the numbers in English. When they had learned to pronounce the words perfectly, they played a real game. As they hopped from square to square, Jennifer said the words in French. Mimi said them in English. Mimi won, but Jennifer didn't mind. She thought she might have a friend at last. And she had learned eight new French words.

Mimi didn't speak to Jennifer for the rest of the day, but she smiled at her every so often. Jennifer was very happy.

The next day at recess Mimi and Jennifer played their game again. Jennifer won four games. Mimi won two. By the time they were through, they each knew their numbers very well. They couldn't wait until that evening to tell their families.

That night it rained. The next day when Jennifer and Mimi came out for recess, their game was almost gone.

Jennifer ran inside and got another piece of chalk. Then she began to draw. When she was through, the game looked like this:

When Mimi saw what Jennifer had drawn, she began to smile. Then she took the chalk and wrote the words in French, so that the game looked like this:

Then she pronounced the words carefully so that Jennifer could learn them.

Jennifer did the same with the English words. Before long the girls were able to pronounce the words perfectly in English and French.

Then they began to play. Jennifer won the first game, and then it was time to go inside.

Throughout the fall, Jennifer worked very hard to learn to speak French. And Mimi, having found that learning English can be fun, worked even harder.

By the time winter came to Paris, Jennifer and Mimi had learned about a hundred new words by playing hopscotch. So they were able to speak to each other. Their words were sometimes in English and sometimes in French, but they each knew what the other meant——and that was all that mattered.

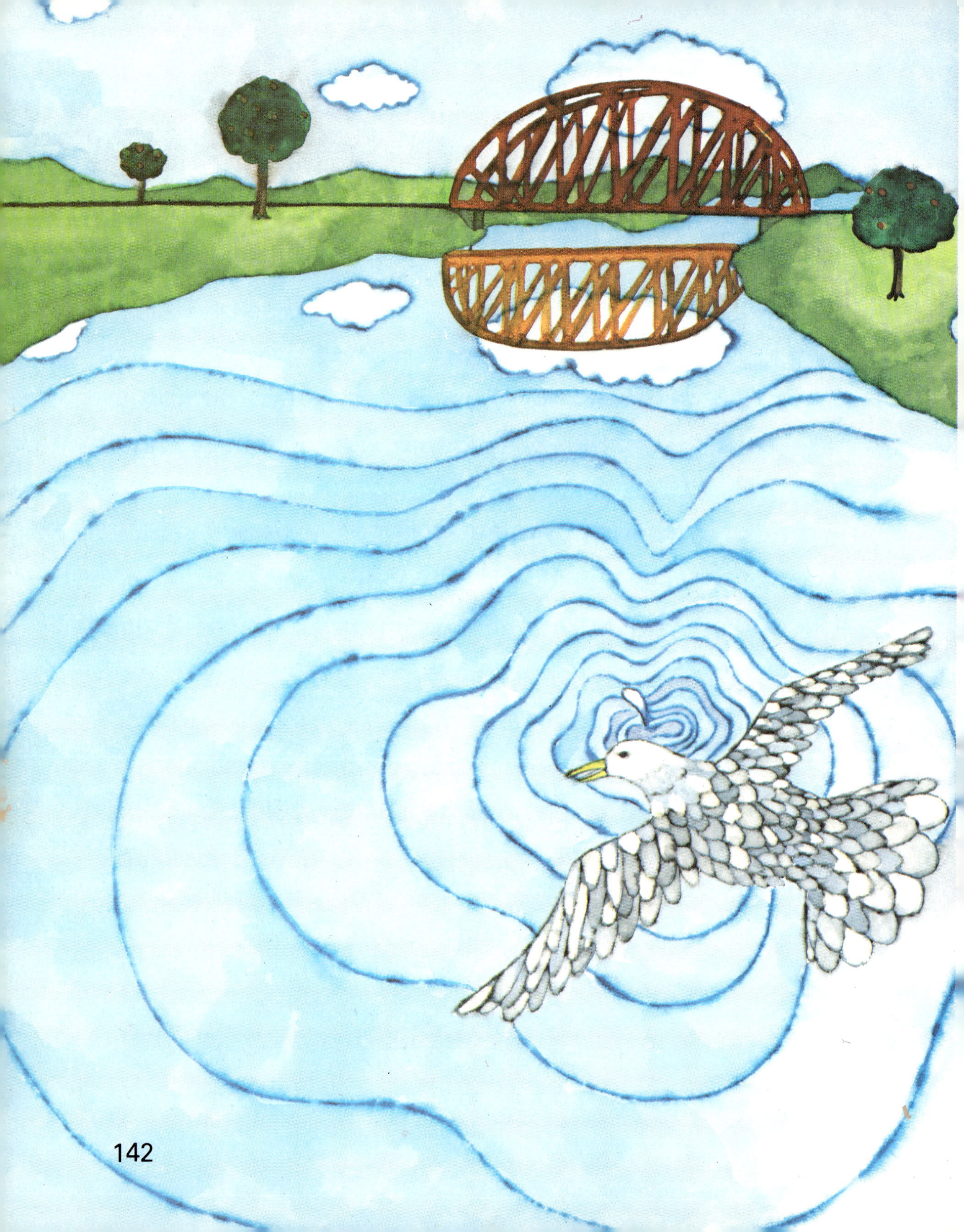

The River Is a Piece of Sky

From the top of a bridge
The river below
Is a piece of sky—
    Until you throw
    A penny in
    Or a cockle shell
    Or a pebble or two
    Or a cobblestone
    Or a fat man's cane—
And then you can see
It's a river again.

The difference you'll see
When you drop your penny:
The river has splashes.
The sky hasn't any.

—John Ciardi

The Girl Who Found a Dragon

Darlene Geis

Mary Anning lived in an English seaside village. Her father used to hunt for fossil shells, which he sold to the summer visitors. From the time Mary was five years old, her father used to take her with him. There were many fossils to be found on the cliffs and beaches outside the town.

When Mary was ten years old, her father died. But she carried on the hard and dangerous work herself. She was only a child but she knew a lot about fossils.

Then one day in 1811, when she was only twelve years old, Mary Anning made one of the great discoveries of her time. She found her first "dragon." It was a skeleton of fossil bones in a blue slate layer of the cliff. There it lay, almost seven feet long!

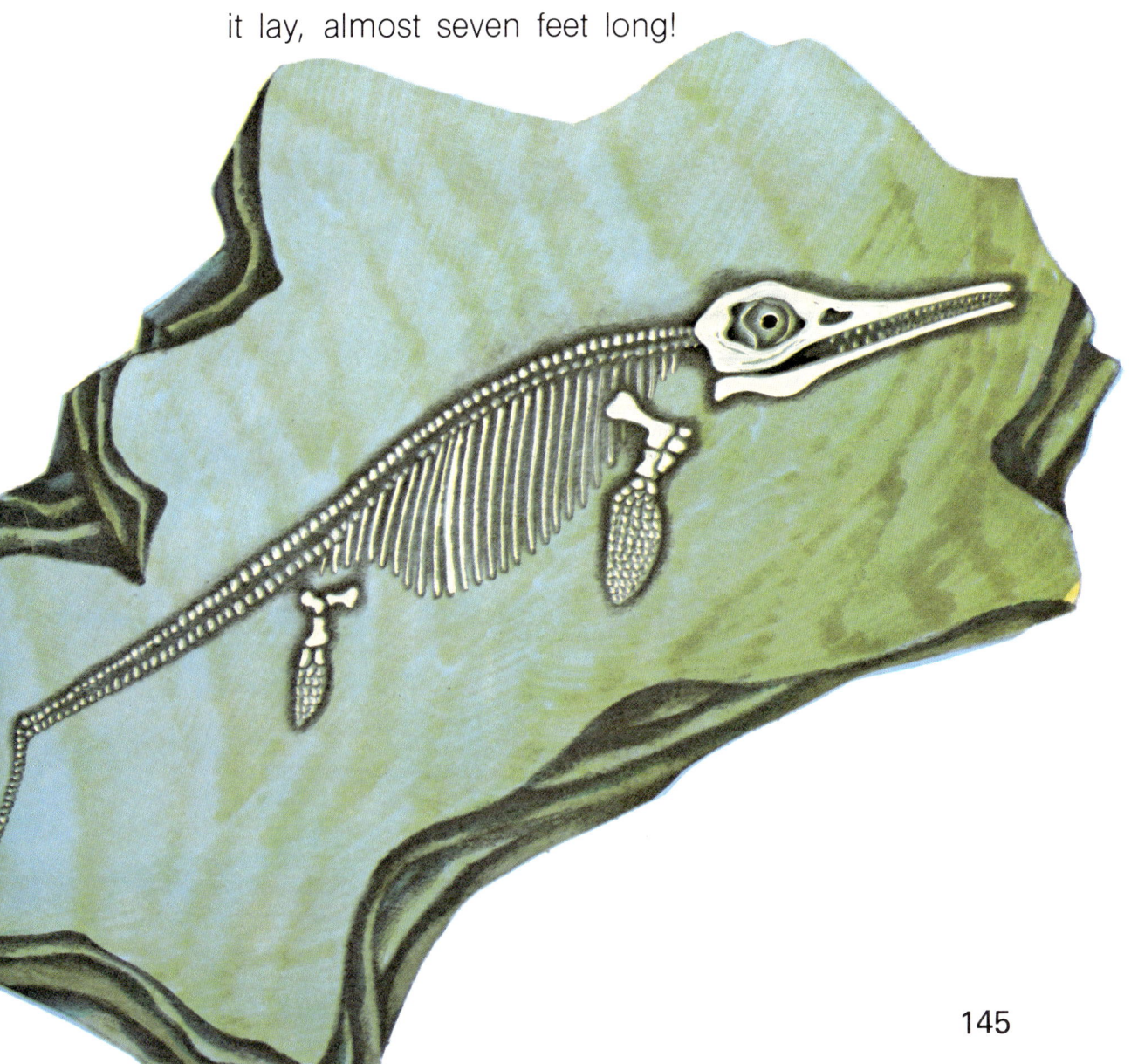

Some men from the village helped Mary pry the stone loose from the cliff. She saw at once that her dragon was not just something to be sold to the summer people. So she had it taken to a very important man. He paid her more than one hundred dollars for it.

He sent it to a museum. Scientists from all over the world studied the fossil dragon. Mary Anning collected fossils for scientists from then on. Once a king even came to her shop and bought a fossil from her.

Mary learned about the different rock layers in the cliff, too. She learned which ones might hold the fossils she wanted. Later, she found the fossil of a kind of sea snake. Then some years after that, Mary made her third great discovery. It was the skeleton of a flying reptile. It was the first to be found in England.

Scientists all over the world knew of Mary's work. They were very excited about her fossils. When Mary first found the skeleton of the dragon in the cliffs near her home, she had no idea what it was. Even the scientists knew little about the creature.

In fact, the scientists studied it for seven years before naming it. It seemed to be half fish and half lizard. Finally, the scientists put together the Greek names for fish and lizard. They made the name *ichthyosaur*. Over the years, they have come to understand the story of the reptile. The reptile had crawled back into the sea and become almost like a large fish.

Mary Anning's dragon was a puzzle to scientists, because only the skeleton was there. The skeleton looked like a lizard with a long thin tail (which seemed to be broken and bent near the end). It had a long snout with hundreds of teeth and very large eyes. It had two large front paddles and two tiny rear ones. The scientists tried to find out what the dragon must have looked like. They drew a shape around its bones. It turned out to look very much like a lizard.

Then a very famous scientist became excited about the drawing. He noticed those large front paddles. "Very like a whale," he thought. But whales have no back paddles at all. Instead, they have a very large tail fin with which they move through the water. Their large paddles are only for steering.

The scientist decided that a creature the size of the ichthyosaur must have had a tail fin, too. But since fins have no bones, they would not show up in a skeleton. He guessed that the tail fin would have had strong muscles linking it to the backbone. Such bones always have marks to show where muscles were attached to them.

Sure enough, the ichthyosaur bones had such marks. So the long lizard-like tail bone had really had a large fin attached to it. The fossil backbone had not been broken or bent. It grew down at the end to hold the bottom fin. Now the ichthyosaur was beginning to look more like a fish.

Some years later, another scientist was working on an ichthyosaur skeleton that was in a piece of slate. In order to get at the old bones, the slate had to be chipped and pried off very carefully.

While this scientist was working on the skeleton, he upset a glass of water on the piece of slate. When the water dried, it left a dark shape around the bones that looked like a giant fish! There it was, a beautiful creature, with the long snout, a big tail fin, and—most surprising of all—a sail-shaped fin on top to its back.

That is how, through hard work and a bit of luck, scientists found out what the dragon really looked like. It had been a great puzzle. No one could have guessed how closely this reptile had come to look like a fish because of living a fish's life.

Later ichthyosaur skeletons showed that the mother hatched her eggs inside her body. The baby ichthyosaurs were born alive. Little by little, the whole wonderful story of this water monster was pried from the rocks.

FAMOUS

from *The Guinness Book of World Records*

HERE ARE SOME WORLD RECORDS, JUST WAITING TO BE BROKEN!

TREE CLIMBING
The record for climbing a tree is held by a woman. She climbed a ninety-foot pine tree in thirty-six seconds.

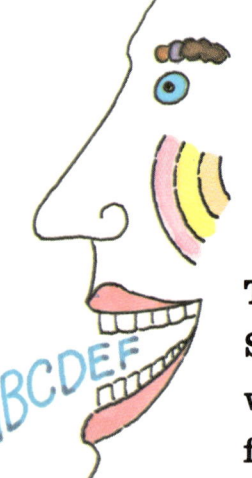

TALKING
Someone talked without stopping for six days and four minutes!

CLAPPING
Two teenagers hold the record for clapping. They clapped, without stopping, for more than fifty-eight hours.

FIRSTS

STONE SKIPPING
A person made a stone skip across water twenty-four times with just one throw!

ROLLER COASTING
The record for roller coasting is held by three people. They stayed on a roller coaster for 100 hours. They covered 1,411.2 miles.

WALKING ON HANDS
A man once walked 871 miles on his hands. He walked ten hours a day for fifty-five days.

Watch Out!

Some words look alike because they are spelled alike. But these words may not sound alike or have the same meaning. You have to read how the word is used in a sentence. Then you will know how to say the word, and you will know what it means.

Roberto's birthday present is a new bike.
We will present a play about Abe Lincoln.

In the first sentence, *present* means "a gift someone gives to someone else." In the second sentence, *present* means "to show something or someone."

Read each set of word meanings. Then read each numbered sentence. Choose the right meaning for each underlined word. Write that meaning on your paper.

Set A
To bow is to bend your body forward.
A bow is a piece of cloth tied in loops.

1. She put a large blue <u>bow</u> on the present.
   1. A bow is a piece of cloth tied in loops.
2. You should <u>bow</u> to the queen.
3. His apron had a <u>bow</u> at the back.

Set B

The <u>wind</u> is air moving quickly.
To <u>wind</u> is to wrap something in the shape of a circle.

1. <u>Wind</u> up the rope when you have finished using it.
2. The <u>wind</u> blew the nest out of the tree.

Set C

A <u>desert</u> is land with hardly any water.
To <u>desert</u> is to leave someone or something.

1. The sailors did not <u>desert</u> the ship.
2. Only a few plants can live in a <u>desert</u>.

Set D

To be <u>close</u> is to be very near something.
To <u>close</u> is to shut something.

1. A big spider sat much too <u>close</u> to me.
2. It's very cold, so let's <u>close</u> the door.

Simon Boom Gives A Wedding

Yuri Suhl

Part One

Only the Best

Once there was a man named Simon Boom who liked to brag: "I buy only the best." It didn't matter if the best was a size too short, or a size too long, or altogether out of season. If it was the best, Simon Boom bought it.

One summer day Simon Boom walked into a hat store. He said to the storekeeper, "Give me the best hat you have."

"Very well," said the storekeeper. He brought out the best straw hat in the store.

"Is this the best you have?" said Simon Boom.

"I have a still better hat," said the storekeeper. "But it's made of felt."

"I don't want a better hat," Simon Boom said. "I want the best hat."

"Very well," said the storekeeper. "The very best hat I have is made of wool. It will keep your head warm on the coldest day."

"If it is the very best, I'll buy it," said Simon Boom. And he did.

That summer all the people in town felt cool in their light hats. Only Simon Boom was hot in his heavy winter hat.

"My head feels so warm," thought Simon Boom. "I'll buy myself an umbrella to hide it from the sun." And so he walked into an umbrella store. He said to the storekeeper, "Give me the best umbrella you have."

"Beach umbrella, or rain umbrella?" the storekeeper asked.

"Best umbrella," said Simon Boom.

"Very well," said the storekeeper. She pulled a black umbrella out of the umbrella stand and opened it up. "This is the best I have," she said. "It's very strong. If it doesn't keep the rain off of you, your money will be returned at once."

"If it's the best, I'll buy it," said Simon Boom. And he did.

Now Simon Boom was the only person in town wearing a winter hat and carrying an open rain umbrella on a bright summer day.

The umbrella didn't help much and Simon Boom thought, "I'll buy myself a light suit to keep cool." And so he walked into a clothing store. He said to the storekeeper, "Give me the best suit you have."

"What kind would you like?" asked the storekeeper.

"The best," Simon Boom answered.

"Very well," said the storekeeper. He brought out a fine tweed suit. "This is made of the finest wool. It will keep you warm on the coldest day. But it may be a little too large for you. What size do you wear?"

"I wear a 38 short," said Simon Boom.

"This suit is a 42 long," the storekeeper said. "And it's the only one left. I'm sorry."

"If it's the best, I'll buy it," Simon Boom said. And he did.

Now Simon Boom was the only person in town wearing a warm winter hat, a warm winter suit, and carrying an open umbrella on a bright summer day.

Simon Boom had a daughter named Rosalie. The time came for Rosalie to get married. Simon Boom said to his wife, "Our daughter is starting out on a new life. I am going to give her the best wedding party ever held in this town. I'll ask the best people and serve the best food. It will be a wedding party the whole town will talk about. I want nothing but the best for my daughter, Rosalie."

"What shall we serve our guests," his wife asked, "fish or chicken?"

"Fish," said Simon Boom. "All kinds of fish. Bluefish, whitefish, cod, and lots more."

Three days before the wedding Simon Boom went to see the fish dealer. "I will need two hundred pounds of the very best fish for my daughter's wedding," he said to the fish dealer. "All kinds of fish."

"Very well," said the fish dealer. "You shall have all the fish you want."

"But I want the best fish," Simon Boom said.

"Our fish are as sweet as sugar," said the fish dealer.

"Did you say sweet as sugar?" Simon Boom asked.

"Upon my word, sir," the fish dealer said. "Sweet as sugar."

"Aha," thought Simon Boom to himself. "If he said sweet as sugar, then sugar must be better than fish. I shall get sugar instead." And so he said to the fish dealer, "I have changed my mind," and he left.

Simon Boom went straight to the sugar merchant. He said, "I will need two hundred pounds of sugar for my daughter's wedding."

"Very well, sir," said the sugar merchant. "You shall have all the sugar you want."

"But I want the very *best* sugar," Simon Boom told the man.

"Our sugar is as sweet as honey," said the sugar merchant.

"Did you say sweet as honey?" Simon Boom asked.

"Upon my word, sir," the sugar merchant said, "sweet as honey."

"Aha," Simon Boom thought to himself. "If he said sweet as honey, then honey must be better than sugar. I shall get honey instead." And so he said to the sugar merchant, "I have changed my mind," and walked away.

Simon Boom went straight to the honey merchant. He said, "I want two hundred jars of honey for my daughter's wedding."

"Very well," said the honey merchant, "You shall have all the honey you want."

"But I want the very *best* honey you have," Simon Boom said.

"Our honey is as clear as oil," said the honey merchant.

"Did you say clear as oil?" Simon Boom asked.

"Upon my word, sir," said the honey merchant, "clear as oil."

"Aha," Simon Boom thought to himself. "If she said clear as oil, then oil must be better than honey. I shall get oil instead." And so he said to the honey merchant, "I have changed my mind," and he left.

Simon Boom then went straight to the oil merchant. He said, "I want two hundred quarts of oil for my daughter's wedding."

"Very well, sir," said the oil merchant. "You shall have all the oil you want."

"But I want the very *best* oil," Simon Boom said.

"Our oil is as pure as spring water," said the oil merchant.

"Did you say pure as spring water?" Simon Boom asked.

"Upon my word, sir," the oil merchant said, "as pure as spring water."

"Aha," Simon Boom thought to himself. "If he said as pure as spring water, then spring water must be better than oil. I shall get spring water instead." And so he said to the oil merchant, "I have changed my mind," and he left.

Part Two

The Very Best

Simon Boom walked all over town looking for a spring-water store. He couldn't find one. He was about to give up when he saw the water carrier. He had two wooden cans of water hanging from the yoke on his back. "Maybe he would know," Simon Boom thought to himself. "He deals in water." And so he ran up to the water carrier and said, "Could you please tell me where I can buy some spring water?"

"Of course I can," said the water carrier, putting his two cans down on the ground.

"At last!" said Simon Boom, feeling much happier now. "I have been looking for that spring-water store all over town and couldn't find it."

"No wonder!" said the water carrier. "The water you are looking for is not in a store. It's in a well."

"But I want spring water," said Simon Boom, "not well water."

"My dear sir," said the water carrier, "well water is the purest, coolest spring water there is."

"Is it also the *best*?" Simon Boom asked.

"The very best," said the water carrier.

"If it is the very best," said Simon Boom, "then I want twenty barrels of it for my daughter's wedding."

"You shall have all the well water you want," said the water carrier. "When is the wedding taking place?"

"In three days," said Simon Boom.

"I'll bring it over just before the guests arrive so the water will be fresh and cool," the water carrier told Simon Boom.

When Simon Boom came home, his wife said, "You look happy. That means you got the fish you wanted."

"Not fish and not sugar either," said Simon Boom.

"You bought chicken instead?"

"Not chicken and not honey either," said Simon Boom.

"You bought meat instead?"

"Not meat and not oil either," Simon Boom said.

"Then what **did** you buy?" his wife wanted to know.

"I bought something that is sweeter than sugar, clearer than honey, purer than oil, and better than all three of them."

"Doesn't it have a name?" his wife asked.

"It has," said Simon Boom. "The Best."

"The best what?"

"That, my dear wife, I want to be a surprise even to you," said Simon Boom.

"But will it come in time for me to cook it?" his wife asked.

"It doesn't have to be cooked," Simon Boom said.

"It doesn't have to be cooked? My, that **is** a surprise."

"It's the Best," said Simon Boom, smiling happily.

A few hours before the wedding party was to begin, Mrs. Boom ordered the servants to set the table. Simon Boom walked into the dining room and saw what they were doing. He shouted to the servants, "Off with the plates! Off with the forks! Off with the spoons! Only the glasses will stay!"

Just then Simon Boom's wife walked into the dining room. When she saw what was happening, she was very upset. "I ordered the table set," she told the servants.

"And I ordered it unset," Simon Boom told her. "For my special dish all we need is glasses."

"Not even plates, and forks, and spoons?" his wife said. "This **is** a surprise!"

"The Best," said Simon Boom, smiling happily again.

The water carrier kept his promise. Shortly before the guests began to arrive, he rolled the twenty barrels of well water up the hill to Simon Boom's house. As soon as Rosalie was married, Simon Boom ordered the servants to fill every pitcher in the house with water from the barrels. Then the pitchers were placed all around the table.

It was a warm evening. As soon as the guests arrived, they filled their glasses and drank. "Ah," they said, "fresh, cold water! That's just what we need."

"See how they love it?" said Simon Boom to his wife. "That's because we are serving the Best! The very Best." And he ordered the servants to keep the pitchers full.

Soon the musicians struck up a happy wedding tune. The guests began to dance. When the dance was over, the guests were warm and ready for something to drink.

They went back to the table for some fresh, cold water. Simon Boom watched them fill up their glasses. He said to his wife, "You see what happens when you serve the Best? They love it."

Now the guests were beginning to get hungry. They waited for food. But all they got was more water. They filled their glasses and drank it. "Look how they drink it!" said Simon Boom to his wife. "They just don't seem to get enough of that wonderful well water."

The musicians struck up another lively tune. But the guests were now too hungry to get up and dance. So they sat at the table. They drank some more water to keep their stomachs from rumbling. "Our guests must be pretty hungry by now," said Mrs. Boom to her husband. "All we have been giving them is water. Don't you think we should give them something to eat, too?"

"Of course not!" said Simon Boom. "We are serving the Best, and there is nothing better than the Best."

By twelve o'clock the guests were so full of water that they couldn't even keep their eyes open. They all fell asleep at the table.

"Maybe if they had some food they might be able to stay awake," said Mrs. Boom.

"What they need is some more of that fresh, cold water to wake them up," said Simon Boom. And he ordered the servants to fill up all the glasses.

"Sorry," said the servants, "but the pitchers are empty."

"Then fill up the pitchers!" Simon Boom shouted loudly.

"Sorry," said the servant, "but the barrels, too, are empty."

"Then fill up the barrels!" Simon Boom ordered the servants. "Roll them down to the well and fill them up. Hurry! Hurry! Hurry!" he shouted.

The guests were awakened by Simon Boom's shouting. They thought that, at last, the food was about to be served.

"I have something to say," Simon Boom said. "I know that you would all like to have some of that fresh, cool well water. And you shall have it! I just sent my servants to the well. They will soon return with twenty more barrels of the same water, the Best."

When the guests heard the news that more water was coming, they all got up and made for the door. In a few minutes they were all gone.

"Now look what you have done!" Mrs. Boom said to her husband. "I'll never live down the shame," she cried. "Won't you **ever** listen to me? Imagine, serving only water at my daughter's wedding party!"

"Only water!" Simon Boom shouted. "But what kind of water? I served them water that is:

sweeter than sugar,
clearer than honey,
purer than oil,
and better than all three of them.
I served them the Best.
The VERY Best!"

Over in the Meadow

Olive A. Wadsworth

Over in the meadow,
In the sand, in the sun,
Lived an old mother-toad
And her little toadie one.
"Wink!" said the mother;
"I wink," said the one.
So she winked and she blinked
In the sand, in the sun.

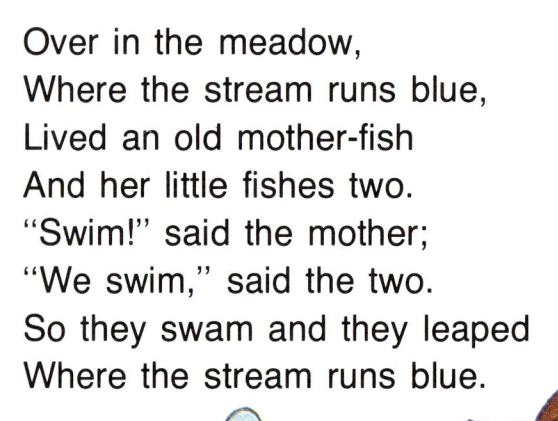

Over in the meadow,
Where the stream runs blue,
Lived an old mother-fish
And her little fishes two.
"Swim!" said the mother;
"We swim," said the two.
So they swam and they leaped
Where the stream runs blue.

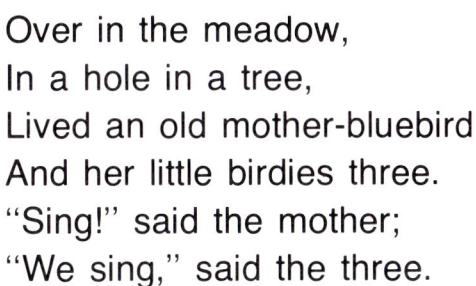

Over in the meadow,
In a hole in a tree,
Lived an old mother-bluebird
And her little birdies three.
"Sing!" said the mother;
"We sing," said the three.
So they sang and were glad
In the hole in the tree.

Over in the meadow,
In the reeds on the shore,
Lived an old mother-muskrat
And her little ratties four.
"Dive!" said the mother;
"We dive," said the four.
So they dived and they burrowed
In the reeds on the shore.

Over in the meadow,
In a snug beehive,
Lived a mother-honeybee
And her little bees five.
"Buzz!" said the mother;
"We buzz," said the five.
So they buzzed and they hummed
In the snug beehive.

Over in the meadow,
In a nest built of sticks,
Lived a black mother-crow
And her little crows six.
"Caw!" said the mother;
"We caw," said the six.
So they cawed and they called
In the nest built of sticks.

Over in the meadow,
Where the grass is so even,
Lived a gray mother-cricket
And her little crickets seven.
"Chirp!" said the mother;
"We chirp," said the seven.
So they chirped cheery notes
In the grass soft and even.

Over in the meadow,
By the old mossy gate,
Lived a brown mother-lizard
And her little lizards eight.
"Bask!" said the mother;
"We bask," said the eight.
So they basked in the sun
By the old mossy gate.

Over in the meadow,
Where the clear pools shine,
Lived a green mother-frog
And her little froggies nine.
"Croak!" said the mother;
"We croak," said the nine.
So they croaked and they splashed
Where the clear pools shine.

Over in the meadow,
In a sly little den,
Lived a gray mother-spider
And her little spiders ten.
"Spin!" said the mother;
"We spin," said the ten.
So they spun lace webs
In the sly little den.

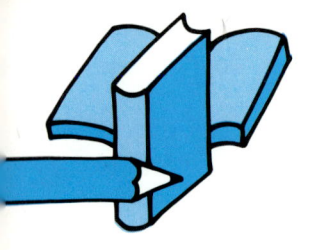

Before and After

Read the lists below.

un- not	**-ful** full of
<u>un</u>real — not real	hope<u>ful</u> — full of hope
re- again	**-er** one who can
<u>re</u>run — run again	danc<u>er</u> — one who dances

ACTIVITY A   Write the words below on your paper. Then write the meaning of each word.

Set 1

1. redo   1. redo — do again
2. replace   3. reclean   4. unlucky
5. unsafe   6. unhappy   7. reuse

Set 2

1. fearful   2. teacher   3. helpful
4. painter   5. careful   6. player

ACTIVITY B   Read the sentences on the next page. Look at the underlined word in each sentence. On your paper, write the meaning of the underlined word.

1. It was <u>unfair</u> not to let everyone go.
   1. unfair — not fair
2. The police had to <u>reopen</u> the case.
3. This box of crayons is <u>unused</u>.
4. You need to <u>rebuild</u> your sand castle.
5. The dog was very angry, but Mindy was <u>unafraid</u>.
6. The glass is broken, so we will have to <u>replace</u> it.
7. Please <u>unlock</u> the door and let the cat in.
8. We need a <u>writer</u> for the new book.
9. The music in the restaurant was very <u>restful</u>.
10. Ann's report on animals was very <u>meaningful</u>.
11. Do you think the <u>pitcher</u> is the most important baseball player?
12. Harry is the best <u>jumper</u> in school.
13. On the day of the picnic, we were <u>thankful</u> for the lovely sunshine.
14. The baker made a <u>beautiful</u> wedding cake.

BEGINNINGS

It's not always easy to start doing things in a new way. Sometimes the old way to do something is a good way to do it. Other times, it's just more comfortable not to change. But you should look for better ways to do things.

Thinking About "Beginnings"

1. Why did Mrs. K. have to find something to do about Mr. Lincoln's crowing?
2. How would "Hot Enough for You?" be different if Erica and her friends lived in the country?
3. What gift did Margarita give Barbara?
4. What was special about the cliffs and beaches near Mary Anning's village?
5. Why didn't the way Simon Boom looked for only the best work very well?
6. What better ways can you think of to do some of the things you do?

Glossary

This glossary will help you to pronounce and to understand the meanings of some of the unusual or difficult words in this book.

The pronunciation of each word is printed beside the word in this way: **o·pen** (ō′pən). The letters, signs, and key words in the list below will help you read the pronunciation respelling. When an entry word has more than one syllable, a dark accent mark (′) is placed after the syllable that has the heaviest stress. In some words, a light accent mark (′) is placed after the syllable that receives a less heavy stress.

The pronunciation key, syllable breaks, accent mark placements, and phonetic respellings in this glossary are adapted from the Macmillan *Beginning Dictionary* (1981) and the Macmillan *School Dictionary* (1981). Other dictionaries may use other pronunciation symbols.

Pronunciation Key

a	bad	hw	white	ô	off	th	that	ə *stands for*
ā	cake	i	it	o͝o	wood	u	cup	a *as in* ago
ä	father	ī	ice	o͞o	food	ur	turn	e *as in* taken
b	bat	j	joke	oi	oil	yo͞o	music	i *as in* pencil
ch	chin	k	kit	ou	out	v	very	o *as in* lemon
d	dog	l	lid	p	pail	w	wet	u *as in* helpful
e	pet	m	man	r	ride	y	yes	
ē	me	n	not	s	sit	z	zoo	
f	five	ng	sing	sh	ship	zh	treasure	
g	game	o	hot	t	tall			
h	hit	ō	open	th	thin			

185

A

a·bil·i·ty (ə bil′ə tē) *n.* talent or skill.

ac·tu·al·ly (ak′chōō ə lē) *adv.* in fact; really.

ad·mir·er (ad mīr′ər) *n.* a person who thinks someone or something is very good or very beautiful.

ar·rive (ə rīv′) *v.* **ar·rived, ar·riv·ing.** to reach a place by traveling; to come.

at·tach (ə tach′) *v.* to fasten to or on; join; connect.

B

bar·rel (bar′əl) *n.* a large wooden container shaped like a cylinder, usually made of boards held together by metal hoops.

bean·curd (bēn′curd′) *n.* pressed, puréed soybeans, usually sold in white, custardlike squares, and eaten extensively in the Orient.

bee·hive (bē′hīv′) *n.* a hive or house for a colony of bees.

bi·cy·cle (bī′si kəl) *n.* a light vehicle to ride on. A bicycle has two wheels, one behind the other; a seat; handlebars; and two foot pedals.

booth (bōōth) *n.* a stall for the display or sale of goods.

bor·der (bôr′dər) *n.* a boundary line.

bur·row (bur′ō) *v.* to dig a hole in which to live or hide.

C

calm (käm) *adj.* free from excitement or strong feeling; quiet; serene.

cam·er·a (kam′ər ə, kam′rə) *n.* a device for taking photographs or motion pictures.

Car·ni·val (kär′nə vəl) *n.* the period of feasting and merrymaking that comes just before Lent.

cer·e·mo·ni·al (ser′ə mō′nē əl) *adj.* used in connection with a ceremony or some particular occasion.

chat·ter (chat′ər) *v.* to talk rapidly and foolishly, usually about matters of little importance.

chirp (churp) *v.* to make a short, sharp sound, such as that of a bird.

choc·o·late (chô′kə lit, chok′ə lit) *n.* a food made from ground and roasted cacao beans.

clue (kloo) *n.* a guide or key that aids in finding the solution to a problem or mystery.

cock·er span·iel (kok'ər span'yəl) a small dog with a flat or slightly waved dense coat of any of several colors.

code (kōd) *n.* a system of writing used to keep messages secret, in which letters, symbols, or numbers stand for the letters and words of the message.

com·plaint (kəm plānt') *n.* an expression of dissatisfaction.

cos·tume (kos'toom, kos'tyoom) *n.* clothing belonging to another time or place, worn on the stage, at parties, and so on.

cou·sin (kuz'in) *n.* a son or daughter of one's uncle or aunt.

crick·et (krik'it) *n.* a hopping insect related to the grasshopper, having strong hind legs and long slender antennae.

croak (krōk) *v.* to make a deep, hoarse sound.

Cub·ism (kyoo'biz'əm) *n.* a movement in art, especially painting, begun in the early twentieth century, characterized by the use of basic geometric forms to represent objects.

curb (kurb) *n.* a border of concrete, stone, or other material along the edge of a street or sidewalk; outer edge of a sidewalk.

cus·to·di·an (kus tō'dē ən) *n.* a person responsible for the care of a building; janitor.

D

deck (dek) *v.* to dress or adorn; ornament.

de·light (di līt') *v.* to give great pleasure or joy to; please highly.

de·serve (di zurv') *v.* **de·served, de·serv·ing.** to have a right to; to be worthy of; merit.

de·ter·mined (di tur'mind) *adj.* a person showing or having a fixed purpose; having one's mind made up.

dif·fi·cult (dif'ə kult') *adj.* hard to do or perform; demanding effort; not easy.

---

a b**a**d, ā c**a**ke, ä f**a**ther; e p**e**t, ē m**e**; i **i**t, ī **i**ce; o h**o**t, ō **o**pen, ô **o**ff; oo w**oo**d, oo f**oo**d; oi **oi**l, ou **ou**t; th **th**in, th **th**at; u c**u**p, ur t**ur**n, yoo m**u**sic; zh trea**s**ure; ə **a**go, tak**e**n, penc**i**l, lem**o**n, helpf**u**l

disappoint   **guest**

dis·ap·point (dis′ə point′) *v.* to fail to fulfill the hope, desire, or expectation of.

dis·cov·er·y (dis kuv′ə rē) *n. pl.,* **dis·cov·er·ies.** something that is seen or found for the first time.

du·et (dōō et′, dyōō et′) *n.* a musical composition for two voices or instruments.

E

ear·phone (ēr′fōn′) *n.* a receiver held at or worn over the ear to listen.

ech·o (ek′ō) *v.* to be heard again.

em·bar·rass (em bar′əs) *v.* to cause to feel uncomfortable or ashamed.

ex·claim (eks klām′) *v.* to speak or cry out suddenly, as in anger or surprise.

F

fa·mous (fā′məs) *adj.* having great fame; well-known; renowned.

fea·ture (fē′chər) *n.* a story, article, or column of special interest, appearing in a magazine or newspaper.

fig (fig) *n.* a small, sweet fruit having many tiny seeds. Figs grow in the Mediterranean region and in California.

for·tune (fôr′chən) *n.* something that happens or is going to happen to a person, whether good or bad; fate; luck.

fos·sil (fos′əl) *n.* the remains or traces of an animal or plant that lived long ago.

four·teen (fôr′tēn′) *n.* four more than ten.—*adj.* amounting to 14 in number.

G

glance (glans) *v.* **glanced, glanc·ing. 1.** to take a quick look. **2.** to hit something and move off at a slant.

guest (gest) *n.* a person who is received by another, as for a party, meal, or visit.

188

handsome   moment

H

hand·some (han'səm) *adj.* having a pleasing, dignified appearance.

Har·le·quin (här'lə kwin, här'lə kin)

harm (härm) *n.* injury; hurt.

hoo·ray (hoo rā') *interj.* a word used as an exclamation of joy, encouragement, or the like.

hy·drant (hī'drənt) *n.* a street fixture for drawing water directly from a water main, consisting of an upright pipe with spouts to which hoses can be attached.

I

ich·thy·o·saur (ik'thē ə sôr') *n.* any of an extinct group of marine reptiles that resembled fish.

in·tel·li·gent (in tel'ə jənt) *adj.* having or showing intelligence; bright; smart.

in·ter·est·ed (in'tris tid, in'tə res'tid) *adj.* having or showing concern or curiosity.

in·ven·tor (in ven'tər) *n.* a person who makes or invents a new device or process.

K

ki·mo·no (ki mō'nə) *n.* a loose robe or gown that is tied with a sash.

L

la·dy (lā'dē) *n. pl.,* **la·dies.** **1.** any woman. **2.** a woman of high social position. **3.** a girl or woman who is polite or has good manners.

loose (loos) *adj.* not confined; free.

M

mad·ame (mad'əm, mə dam') *n.* a title of respect or form of polite address for a woman.

mad·e·moi·selle (mad'ə mə zel') *n.* miss: a French form of address for an unmarried girl or woman.

mis·er·a·ble (miz'ər ə bəl) *adj.* very unhappy; wretched.

mo·ment (mō'mənt) *n.* a short period of time.

---

a b**a**d, ā c**a**ke, ä f**a**ther; e p**e**t, ē m**e**; i **i**t, ī **i**ce; o h**o**t, ō **o**pen, ô **o**ff; oo w**oo**d, oo f**oo**d; oi **oi**l, ou **ou**t; th **th**in, th **th**at; u c**u**p, ur t**ur**n, yoo m**u**sic; zh trea**s**ure; ə **a**go, tak**e**n, penc**i**l, lem**o**n, helpf**u**l

189

mus·cle (mus′əl) *n.* a body tissue made up of fibers that are used to make the body move.

mus·krat (musk′rat′) *n.* a small animal with dark brown fur. Muskrats live in and near the water.

N

ninth (nīnth) *adj.* next after eighth.

P

par·rot (par′ət) *n.* a tropical bird having a hooked bill, large head, and glossy, colored feathers.

per·form (pər fôrm′) *v.* to carry out; do.

pe·ri·od (pir′ē əd) *n.* a portion of time of a given length or marked by certain events or conditions.

Pi·cas·so, Pa·blo (pi kä′sō, pä′blō)

pi·geon (pij′ən) *n.* any of several wild or domesticated birds with a stout body, small head, and thick, soft feathers.

pi·ña·ta (pēn yä′tə) *n.* a colorfully decorated container. It is filled with fruit and candy and hung from the ceiling to be broken with a stick by a blindfolded child.

pour (pôr) *v.* to flow in a steady stream.

pre·pare (pri per′) *v.* **pre·pared, pre·par·ing.** to make or get ready.

prob·a·bly (prob′ ə blē) *adv.* most likely; in all likelihood.

pro·nounce (prə nouns′) *v.* to make the sound of a letter or word.

prop·er (prop′ər) *adj.* correct or suitable for a certain purpose or occasion.

pry (prī) *v.* **pried, pry·ing.** to move, raise, or pull by force; to get with much effort.

pu·pil (pyoo′pəl) *n.* a person who studies under the direction of an instructor; student.

pure (pyoor) *adj.* not mixed with anything else; not contaminated; clean.

pur·pose (pur′pəs) *n.* the reason for which something is made or done. **on purpose.** not by accident; deliberately.

Q

ques·tion (kwes′chən) *n.* something asked in order to receive a reply or find out something.

R

ra·di·o (rā′dē ō′) *n.* device for receiving radio broadcasts or for sending and receiving messages.

re·al·ize (rē′ə līz′) *v.* **re·al·ized, re·al·iz·ing.** to understand completely.

re·cess (rē′ses, ri ses′) *n.* a period of time in which work or other activity is stopped temporarily.

re·flect (ri flekt′) *v.* **1.** to give back an image of. **2.** to serve to give a particular impression.

rep·tile (rep′til, rep′tīl′) *n.* any of a group of cold-blooded animals with backbones, including lizards, snakes, crocodiles, and turtles.

re·tire (ri tīr′) *v.* **re·tired, re·tir·ing.** to withdraw oneself from public life, business, or active service.

S

sad·ness (sad′nis) *n.* unhappiness, sorrow, or gloom.

Sa·gan (sə gän′)

search (surch) *n.* the act of looking or exploring carefully in order to find something.

sea·son (sē′zən) *n.* one of the divisions of the year (spring, summer, fall, winter), marked by differences in weather, temperature, and hours of daylight.

sev·en-thir·ty (sev′ən thur′tē) *n.* half past seven; 7:30.

sew (sō) *v.* **sewed, sewed** or **sewn, sew·ing.** to make or mend by means of a needle and thread or sewing machine; to fasten or join with stitches.

shy (shī) *adj.* uncomfortable in the presence of others; bashful; timid.

skel·e·ton (skel′ə tən) *n.* the framework of bones supporting the body of animal with a backbone.

slate (slāt) *n.* a fine-grained, bluish-gray rock that splits easily into thin sheets or layers.

sly (slī) *adj.* secret; clever.

---

a **b**a**d**, ā **c**a**k**e, ä **f**a**th**er; e **p**e**t**, ē **m**e; i **i**t, ī **ic**e; o **h**o**t**, ō **op**en, ô **o**ff; oo **w**oo**d**; o͞o **f**oo**d**; oi **oi**l, ou **ou**t; th **th**in, <u>th</u> **<u>th</u>**at; u **c**u**p**, ur **t**ur**n**, yo͞o **m**u**s**ic; zh trea**s**ure; ə **a**go, tak**e**n, penc**i**l, lem**o**n, helpf**u**l

so·fa (sō′fə) *n.* a long, upholstered seat with a back and arms; couch.

spi·der (spī′dər) *n.* a small animal with four pairs of legs, a body that is divided into two parts, and no wings.

splen·did (splen′did) *adj.* impressive, brilliant, or glorious.

sprin·kler (spring′klər) *n.* a device that is used to water gardens and lawns.

sta·tion (stā′shən) *n.* a building or place set up as the headquarters for a business or public service.

stead·y (sted′ē) *adj.* not changing; regular or uniform.

strut (strut) *v.* **strut·ted, strut·ting.** to walk in a vain, pompous, or proud way.

stu·di·o (stoō′dē ō′, styoō′dē ō′) *n.* a place where an artist or a photographer works.

sug·ar (shoog′ ər) *n.* a white or brown sweet substance, usually in the form of small crystals or powder.

sug·gest (səg jest′) *v.* to offer or mention for consideration or action; propose.

T

tease (tēz) *v.* **teased, teas·ing.** to make fun of playfully or mischievously.

the·a·ter (thē′ə tər) *n.* a building or other place where plays, motion pictures, or other entertainments are presented.

toad (tōd) *n.* an animal that is like a frog.

trans·late (trans lāt′, trans′lāt′) *v.* **trans·lated, trans·lat·ing.** to change from one language into another.

tweed (twēd) *n.* a rough fabric usually made from wool, woven with yarns of two or more colors.

twelve (twelv) *n.* two more than ten; 12.—*adj.* amounting to 12 in number.

U

up·ward (up′wərd) *adv.* from a lower to a higher place or position.

use·less (yoōs′lis) *adj.* serving no use; having no purpose.

u·su·al·ly (yoō′zhoō ə lē) *adv.* ordinarily; habitually.

W

Wednes·day (wenz′dē, wenz′dā) *n.* the fourth day of the week.

whose (hoōz) *pron.* the possessive case of *who* and *which*.

wink (wingk) *v.* to close and open one eyelid very quickly.